"I wish my character, an adoptive mom in the film *Go Ah (Orphan)*, had been able to read this book! *Let Us Be Greater* is eye-opening, warmly written with grace and keen knowledge of all sides of the subject. From Michelle Madrid's heart and her deeply personal origin story, the book also is, importantly, filled with tangible exercises to work through the darkness and uncover one's authentic self."

— **Diane Kelber**, actor

"*Let Us Be Greater* is more than a book that takes adoptees on a transformative journey of healing and self-discovery. *Let Us Be Greater* is a personal/spiritual manifesto and an invitation to *thrive* in the face of dual identities, encouraging adoptees to grant themselves permission to step into their power and claim every ounce of their humanity."

— **Regina Louise**, author of *Permission Granted* and *Somebody's Someone*

"A beautifully written, comforting, and validating book that will meet you right where you are on the adoptee healing path. It will take your hand and compassionately support your efforts to heal and make sense of your lived experience. This is a very special book, brimming with useful exercises and practices, saturated in acceptance and wisdom. Highly recommended!"

— **Jeff Brown**, author of *Soulshaping* and *Hearticulations*

"Weaving together deeply personal stories and exercises designed for growth and reflection, Michelle Madrid expertly and lovingly guides you to start the work of mending your disconnected inner child. Whether you are an adoptee or a youth with a lived foster care experience, Madrid is your wing(wo)man, gently lifting you out of the fog and into the light. Let us be greater, indeed."

— **Mira Zimet**, documentary filmmaker

"What's striking in Michelle Madrid when you first meet her is her exceptional level of warmth, compassion, gratitude, and appreciation. And now that I've read *Let Us Be Greater*, I can understand why. Her story is one of sadness and happiness, of confusion and comprehension, of fear yet ultimately of triumph. She skillfully weaves powerful life lessons and exercises throughout that can help every adoptee achieve a smoother path. Indeed, this story is one we can all relate to whether adoptee or not, and I believe it will rightly find its way onto the list of must-reads for anyone seeking to mend the wounds of their childhood and become whole again. An uplifting and wonderful book."

— **Angela Middleton**, MBE, social entrepreneur, mind/body/business coach, author, and podcaster

"*Let Us Be Greater* is a compelling read — personal, compassionate, rich in healing insights. Michelle Madrid's self-healing how-tos are magical. She's a Martha Beck for the adoptees."

— **MiYu**, actor/writer, *Go Ah (Orphan)*

Let Us Be
Greater

Let Us Be
Greater

**A GENTLE, GUIDED PATH
TO HEALING FOR ADOPTEES**

Michelle Madrid

Foreword by Gina Moffa, LCSW

New World Library
Novato, California

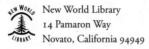

New World Library
14 Pamaron Way
Novato, California 94949

Text design by Tona Pearce Myers

Library of Congress Cataloging-in-Publication Data

Names: Madrid, Michelle, author.
Title: Let us be greater : a gentle, guided path to healing for adoptees / Michelle Madrid.
Description: Novato, California : New World Library, [2023] | Includes bibliographical
    references. | Summary: "A soulful approach to healing the misunderstanding, myth,
    and sense of marginalization within the adoptee community. Through illuminating
    exercises, affirmations, and stories, the book lays out a path that guides adoptees to
    come home to themselves — the greatest reunion of all"-- Provided by publisher.
Identifiers: LCCN 2023023424 (print) | LCCN 2023023425 (ebook) | ISBN
    9781608688470 (paperback) | ISBN 9781608688487 (epub)
Subjects: LCSH: Adoption. | Adoptees. | Marginality, Social.
Classification: LCC HV875 .M337 2023 (print) | LCC HV875 (ebook) |
    DDC 362.734--dc23/eng/20230717
LC record available at https://lccn.loc.gov/2023023424
LC ebook record available at https://lccn.loc.gov/2023023425

First printing, October 2023
ISBN 978-1-60868-847-0
Ebook ISBN 978-1-60868-848-7
Printed in Canada on 100% postconsumer-waste recycled paper

New World Library is proud to be a Gold Certified Environmentally Responsible
Publisher. Publisher certification awarded by Green Press Initiative.

10   9   8   7   6   5   4   3   2   1

For adoptees. Please remember that the external things that have happened to you do not reflect your internal worth and innate deservedness. Because you — in all your shimmering vibrancy — are deserving of deep healing and real happiness.

Only when we are brave enough to explore the darkness will we discover the infinite power of our light.

— Brené Brown

Contents

Foreword

Every day, I witness the immense pain, grief, and trauma people carry around like heavy suitcases from place to place. They are simply longing for a time when they can put it down, open it up, and safely sort through it all with gentleness and tender care. As a psychotherapist in private practice in New York City, I have been privileged to witness all types of losses, but the pain of ambiguous loss — or in its simplest sense, a loss without closure, resolution, or understanding, the kind many adoptees experience — can often feel like the most complicated, confusing, and unrelentingly painful of losses. Endless questions without answers can take a toll. And it can feel so exhausting, you wonder if it will ever feel different. Although I am aware of how deeply sad and heavy that feeling is, I also get to witness moments of revelation that bring healing, joys of all sizes, and immense hope to my clients. I get to be a traveling companion on a journey that reaps endless rewards, and the treasure at the end of the rainbow is finding oneself. In other words, *all along, you have been the pot of gold.*

So, when I was asked to write the foreword to this beautiful book, I was, of course, incredibly humbled and honored, but also excited to be here with you and get to introduce you to Michelle Madrid, someone I find to be among the most exceptional gifts to humanity. Someone about whom I can only speak in superlatives. Someone I trust to be a fellow traveling companion for adoptees and adoptive parents looking for belonging, connection, understanding, peace, forgiveness, and healing — the pots of gold we seek. That's a tall order, I know. But most definitely not insurmountable. Especially within these pages.

As you move forward here, you will be gently guided and sometimes lovingly challenged to look at your life and experiences in different ways, and to learn to reframe your story into one where you can acknowledge and grieve your losses but also celebrate the parts of you that emerge from these losses. You have already shown your courage and innate determination to step forward for yourself simply by opening this book and being here right now. And as you journey through these pages, I encourage you to keep showing up for yourself, keep opening that suitcase and lightening your load. Michelle is a helper, healer, and connector, so I trust that her heart and wisdom here will find their way to you, helping you to sort through all that remains.

Michelle is easy to feel connected to. She and I met by way of a mutual friend and book proposal coach, Richelle Fredson. One day Richelle said to me, "Gina, you have to connect with Michelle Madrid. She has a beautiful heart, and I think you two would really hit it off." So Richelle sent an email to us both, and "really hit it off" is an understatement. It was clear from our first conversation that Michelle was a soul sister. Over the course of the past few years, our friendship has grown to feel like home to me, and I revel in watching her share the intrinsic gift she has for helping people see their own light. I admire her wisdom, tenderness, and warmth, and also her tenacity and courage in the way she shows up to her life, her family, and her work with the adoption community around the globe.

Because of the pandemic, and life moving so fast again, I've yet to meet Michelle in person. But my heart knows her heart. This is the whole point, right? Bonds through space and time. Real connection has no rules, no timeline — well, no sense of time whatsoever, really — and it certainly doesn't have conditions that decide how we get to categorize it. That's not how it works, and I don't know anyone who might understand that concept more deeply than an adoptee. Because she's an international adoptee herself, Michelle's work as a speaker and coach promises to open doors within the hearts of so many who have felt closed off indefinitely. She is such a gentle spirit with a sagacious tenacity, and I am grateful to witness her teach and empower those who feel rejected, abandoned, unwanted, and even betrayed.

As you prepare to delve into the powerful experience of integrating and healing in *Let Us Be Greater*, I invite you to come to it from a lens of openness, curiosity, and hope. That may mean you jump in heart first and face unspoken inner truths. It may mean you set aside time to read this book when you have the bandwidth to *feel and process*, as some of these practices may push you to look at parts of your outer and inner life with a lovingly brutal honesty. Some parts may be like finding a missing puzzle piece that reveals why you've felt a certain feeling your entire life as well as unacknowledged challenges you've faced without understanding what they were about; and some parts may feel like the loving hug you've craved for so many years.

Much like the life of an adoptee (and those who love them), *Let Us Be Greater* is a journey of uncovering, understanding, deeply feeling, grieving, and fully acknowledging the *whole picture* of your life. The stories, exercises, and affirmations remind you that your experiences are valid, that your story matters, and that there is a way through the pain of feeling unwanted or unwelcome in this world, a way through the fog of your grief. The path can feel turbulent or terrifying at times, but all along it, you are surrounded by love — a love that was always there and will *always be there*.

As someone who has witnessed the beauty and insight within this book, and as a therapist who does the work of combing through and integrating grief with those dealing with loss every day, I encourage you to begin reading with the following thoughts tucked away in a pocket of the suitcase for when you may need them:

- You don't have to go this road alone, and you don't have to have anything figured out. This book is a hand in the dark to help guide you home to yourself in new ways.

- However you have responded to your adoptee experience and all that's come with it thus far, your response has been protective and reflexive, showing your intuitive inner strength and not weakness.

- We can't fully heal if we don't allow ourselves the grace of seeing our whole story bathed in the light of truth, self-compassion, and tenderness with ourselves. Complete the exercises in these pages to be as present as you can with your experiences and emotions.

- We are inherently self-protective, so if you feel yourself wanting to run away, that's okay, but when you feel safe again, please come back. Coming back for yourself and your healing is one of the worthiest endeavors. It's the way forward, and Michelle's gentle guidance can feel like shelter in an unpredictable storm.

- You can absolutely rewire and teach your nervous system to find safety, love, and validation in connections, even if you have yet to feel this way in your life or in any relationships.

- Honor the entirety of the feelings that come up for you, even if they include overwhelm, shame, or layer upon layer of grief. Your feelings matter.

- It's okay to grieve for as long as you need to — whether for a home, identity, life, family, milestones, experiences, or countless other unknowns you have never had. Just remember to find the joy, too.

Let this book be a reminder of the good that can accompany the pain. They can and often do coexist.

Let Us Be Greater is a guidepost, a lighthouse, and a steadfast companion. Michelle's compassionate, steady voice will undoubtedly help you find a way toward truth, hope, and, well, *home within*. I don't know you or the experiences you have lived, the story you have to tell, or the ways in which your heart yearns, but I believe in your capacity for healing. If you have picked up this book, I know you are ready to take this journey to reveal your deepest longings, find your truest voice, and receive the gift of remembering how brightly your light shines within you.

Without question or hesitation, I can assure you, you are in the best of hands the entire way.

GINA MOFFA, LCSW, grief and trauma psychotherapist
and author of *Moving On Doesn't Mean Letting Go:*
A Modern Guide to Navigating Loss

Introduction

And, here you are living, despite it all.

— RUPI KAUR

I never would have imagined, as a young international adoptee, that I would one day write a soul-nurturing book guiding readers to heal the pain and confusion of adoption. After all, when I was growing up, the only books I could find on adoption made the experience seem hopeless, clinical, and cold. Instead of feeling supported, I felt lessened and labeled, as if there was something wrong with me — as if I had an ailment that needed to be cured.

In hindsight, perhaps writing this book makes perfect sense. It's a book that I once desperately longed to read — a book built on the foundational belief that every adoptee is a hero: capable of healing their pain, emerging from limiting beliefs, reframing their experiences, and overcoming any obstacle.

The truth is, I didn't see myself as a hero while growing up — far from it! I was placed in the United Kingdom's foster care system as a baby. My foster records stated that I was a matter for the country of England to settle. These words were plainly stated on the documents signed by my mother, relinquishing her right to parent me. Documents that sealed my fate and left me as a ward of the court.

Those foster records contain pages and pages about the earliest parts of my life. My mother, Margaret, named me Julié Dawn, after my father, Juliáno. I was noted as the "extramarital daughter" of the two. I was also labeled by social workers as being — among other things — strange-looking, an ethnic child, illegitimate, and difficult to place due to my darker coloring and undesirable family circumstances. In other words, I wasn't your typical English rose.

None of this reads like the résumé of a hero. For many excruciating years, I felt more like a zero. Diminished. Unwanted. Abandoned. Disempowered. My parents' shameful secret.

I lived with a constant fear of rejection. It was as if this fear had been programmed within me from before I ever took my first breath. My mother contemplated aborting me on three different occasions. She felt the weight of outside pressure from those urging her to abort and spent a great deal of time in counseling as she considered her options.

All along I spent my unborn days just treading the waters of life inside my mother's womb. This isn't meant to be a dramatic statement; it's actually a scientific one. Studies show that unborn children are constantly tuned in to their mother's every action, thought, and feeling. Or, as I like to state — *the adoptee was there*. They experience within the womb what their mother experiences in the world. This is a topic I'll be exploring more in chapter 1.

My mother made the decision to carry me to term, and I arrived into the world on a January morning, in Bury St Edmunds, Suffolk, England. There were no celebrations on the day I was born; no pink balloons and no handing out of cigars with "It's a Girl" ribbons adorning them. I was a baby who was losing her parents. A child feels the slipping away of these parental bonds. It's frightening on a cellular level.

"I don't want to know when the child is born!"

My father shouted these words before he stormed out of my life. This declaration was made during a fiery meeting between my father and my mother's husband. The two men had arranged a face-to-face, in a local pub, to discuss what should happen with my future.

Although Juliáno was normally an easygoing man, he was most unreasonable — even defiant — during the meeting. Tensions mounted in an explosion of words. My mother's husband looked Juliáno in the eyes and said, "If you won't be the father then I will make the decision about what happens to this baby." Juliáno's final reply was to stand up and walk away.

There isn't a lot written about my father in my foster records. I've read or heard only bits and pieces of information, like Juliáno's nickname, "the Spaniard," in the village where he lived. Other insightful notes suggest that Juliáno was a loner, loved reading books on war, had a risk-taking spirit and liked to jump out of planes, and was determined not to take responsibility for me. He didn't want to be my father. He would not be cornered, and his name was not included on my birth certificate.

There was no family member, on either side, willing to take me in. As much as my parents tried, news of Margaret's pregnancy proved hard to keep secret. My teenage sister needed a great deal of support to accept that her mother was having a child by another man. Margaret's father is said to have been "deeply shocked" by his daughter's pregnancy, and he condemned her. My grandfather, whose love of horses would run through my DNA, never wanted to know me, his granddaughter. He was only happy that his wife had passed away before seeing "the shame" that had been placed on his family.

Both my mother and her husband felt that my presence would be a continued stress on their marriage, a constant reminder of her infidelity, and a bone of contention if they had a disagreement of any kind. Margaret made plans to deliver me at a different hospital — away from her normal doctors — so that the family could avoid further embarrassment and gossip.

In the days following my birth, I lost a considerable amount of weight from my initial seven pounds and six ounces. The doctors said that nothing was wrong with me. It is my belief, however, that everything was wrong. How could it not be? I was a baby who knew, inherently, that she was about to lose her mother forever. I believe that the weight loss was due to the immense amount of grief swirling inside me as I awaited the moment when my mother would leave.

After caring for me, cradling me, and even knitting me a few pieces of baby clothing, Margaret placed me into the arms of my foster mother, Mrs. Hopkins. My foster mother was in a state of chaos on the day I was brought to her. There was trouble with a living room chimney, and her home was crawling with workmen. It's written in my foster records that the scene was cold and chaotic. Nevertheless, I was dropped off amid that chaos. My mother left me there, turned around, and walked out of my life.

It was as if everyone involved wanted to erase me from their memory. Only, how can you erase the very people who are a part of you? This is a central question in the adoptee experience. For generations, adoptees have been required to silence essential parts of themselves and to pretend that they don't feel the pulse of their first family — their first heritage — beating within them. This practice of silence and concealment has resulted in a great deal of suffering within the adoptee community. I know this kind of suffering intimately.

Many adoptees have not been permitted to openly grieve their loss. Society is only just beginning to understand what adoptees have always known: that adoption is rooted in loss, that one family must come apart for another family to come together. One relationship must go through a severing for another relationship to be sewn.

Many adoptees express feelings of being erased or made invisible within this loss, as if a part of them has been forced to stop living. From this place of involuntary exile, sadness, anger, hurt, distrust, confusion, and feelings of being unworthy or unlovable can be seeded. The blow of abandonment punches deep into the core of the adoptee's soul, hollowing out much of their earliest identity.

The First Me

I refer to this earliest identity as the "first me." This is the me I was — Julié Dawn — before my adoption. After I'd been adopted by an American couple, my name was changed to Michelle. The girl I had become, postadoption, had a different name, lived in a different country, and had a new set of parents and a completely different set of circumstances. Everything had changed.

I didn't know where to put the first me — Julié Dawn. I quietly mourned her. For years I grieved alone. I tried to work it all out in my mind, but nothing made sense. It was like dying, but not really. It was like living, but not quite. I was existing somewhere in between. This gap can be intensely painful.

Here's something I know for sure — every adoptee has a first chapter, and in that chapter is their first me. These things don't just disappear upon adoption. It doesn't work that way. Every moment of the adoptee's story is relevant. Adoptee Darryl McDaniels, of the legendary rap group Run-DMC, explains it this way: "Every part of your existence, everything that is relevant to you, every experience, every revelation, every piece of your life story is part of your story." Finding harmony in their story, for the adoptee, includes connection with their first chapter and their first me. Adoptees struggle to feel complete, in balance, when they live their life from their second chapter. Every adoptee deserves to connect, in their own way, with their first.

The question to contemplate, and one that is a critical part of the healing journey for adoptees, is, *Where do adoptees place the child they were before adoption happened in their life? That child still exists within them and is an essential part of their chapter one.* It's imperative that we support adoptees as they begin to merge the gap between their first chapter and all the chapters that follow. Adoptees are capable of merging that gap!

I believe that adoptees should never feel guilty about openly grieving the loss of their first identity or first family. They must safely feel their loss and pain in order to move forward. Just as I have mourned losing my first family, I have also mourned the loss of the first me. I have held sacred space for Julié Dawn. I have spoken her name out loud. I've connected with her from a spiritual space and built a bridge back to my first me. I've allowed Julié Dawn to emerge from a place of exile deep within. This process of emerging is where what feels hollow is made complete. It's where what feels lost is finally found.

It is essential for every adoptee to honor this part of who they are — to keep their first me alive in whatever way they see fit along the journey of becoming whole. Adoptees no longer have to live severed from the truth of themselves. When adoptees are separated from their truth, what I call their "pain points" becomes magnified.

Adoptee Pain Points

As an international adoptee and someone who has worked with adopted adults and youth as a life coach, I've identified eight adoptee pain points, places of hurt that adoptees need to heal. These pain points can cause challenges in the adoptee's life, keeping them from a place of peace and wholeness within. Setting the course to compassionately and soulfully heal and reframe these eight primary sources of pain — transforming points of pain into points of light — is the focus of this book. The adoptee pain points are:

1. The pain of feeling unwelcome in the world
2. The pain of broken bonds and a deep sense of loss

3. The pain of being denied access to truth
4. The pain of familial rejection and of words that harm
5. The pain of distrust
6. The pain of banished biology
7. The pain of pleasing others versus pleasing the self
8. The pain of lack of transparency and acceptance

Adoptees may feel out of control and at the mercy of one, several, or all of these pain points. Our work here, together, is to transform this pain and to empower our lives as adoptees.

The motivation to transform can be found in this question:
What if this is as good as it gets?

Is this what you're asking yourself as an adoptee about the pain you're carrying? Do you believe that the pain will never get any better? I learned, through an exercise called the Dickens Process, to sink into a painful limiting belief and imagine what it would feel like if I was still living with it one year, three years, five years, or ten years down the road. The Dickens Process is an NLP (neurolinguistic programming) technique that guides you to use your conscious mind in identifying the consequences of a limiting belief and in deciding whether you want to continue with that belief. The essence of this exercise is based on the character Scrooge from Charles Dickens's *A Christmas Carol.* Scrooge is famously shown his past, his present, and what his future will look like if he doesn't change his ways. The Dickens Process has you identify a limiting belief and then look at it in depth through the lens of three questions:

1. What did this limiting belief cost you and your loved ones in the past? What have you lost because of this belief? See it. Hear it. Feel it.
2. What is this limiting belief costing you and those you care about in the present? See it. Hear it. Feel it.
3. What will this limiting belief cost you and the people

you care about one year, three years, five years, or ten years down the road? See it. Hear it. Feel it.

Once you've dwelled on the pain of this limiting belief and experienced what it feels like to hold on to it, you will be motivated to create a new limitless belief that inspires and empowers you. Here's my question for you:

What limiting belief is holding you back today? What if the pain you feel right now, because of this belief, is exactly how you'll feel one year, three years, five years, or ten years down the road? Maybe you're telling yourself, as I once did, that you're just one of those people meant to live a life that's smaller than the dreams you hold inside. Maybe you believe that staying quiet and concealed, as an adoptee, is how you'll stay safe from rejection. Maybe you're living on someone else's terms. Are you? Are you living someone else's narrative for your life? Are you falling in line but secretly falling apart inside? I don't want you to feel this way — not for one more second. What would it be like for you to leave your limiting beliefs behind, once and for all, and move forward with new and limitless ones? Take time to consider the questions of the Dickens Process. It's a game changer. It works! We'll revisit this process in chapter 1 during a reflection exercise.

My adoptive mother once told me that I could start finding out more about my first family and my ethnicity once she was no longer around. This was a damaging comment, and it came from my own mother. The comment was based in fear, only I didn't know that at the time. Mom was fearful of losing me, and I was petrified of being rejected by her. Neither one of us was operating from a space of unconditional love.

And so I did what my mother asked. Like a good adopted girl, I sat inside the waiting room of my own life. The only thing that grew during that time were the pain points. Like thick vines, they entangled me in fear. I felt trapped and lost. Maybe you do, too.

We're not here, as adoptees, to live someone else's life. We're here to live our own lives, our big and beautiful lives! We're here to be who we are and who we're destined to become. We're here to do that from the purest place of authenticity and essence.

My desire to get to the truth of me and to reignite the light within me has taken me on a transformational journey of self-discovery, self-compassion, and self-love. That journey began when I picked up a book by Louise Hay in graduate school called *You Can Heal Your Life*. The title didn't say that you can heal your life — unless you're adopted. No, it offered me the assurance that I really could heal my life, even as an adoptee. Hay's book awakened me to a place of pure love, empowerment, and self-acceptance. I wanted to get to that place in my own way and through my own experiences. I want to help you get there, too.

My potential once seemed so limited. Today I view my potential as vast and without boundaries. I used to perceive adoption as my weakness, but now I see it as a source of my strength. I've traveled deep within in order to transform my life. I've learned to shift limiting beliefs into limitless truth. I'll be asking you to do the same as we, adoptee to adoptee, move through the pages of this book.

You see, the pain you may be struggling with right now *isn't* as good as it gets. It's not all there is! There's so much more awaiting you beyond the pain. Do you have the power to heal your life? Yes, I believe with all that I am that you do.

The Journey Home

There's no question that adoption is a lifelong journey. The experience of being adopted does not end when the paperwork is signed and the process is finalized. For the adoptee, the process offers many twists and turns, hellos and goodbyes, entries and exits, along the path of finding a way back to connection after separation.

Like so many hard experiences, being adopted is about quieting the voices — around us and within us — that try to diminish the truth of who we are, the worth we possess, and the dreams we hold.

Adoptees have a deep desire to live transparently. Perhaps, more than anyone else, adoptees crave the unvarnished truth. They know, innately, that the truth lives within them. They want to unleash their truth, but the pain points have a chokehold on them. The pain and fear keep them in the waiting room. I want to help you walk boldly through the waiting room exit!

The most powerful way that I've learned to heal the pain is to face it, call it by its name, explore it, understand it, and move through it. Pain point by pain point. Step-by-step. I understand now that living as a prisoner of pain will never bring peace or fulfillment. And peace and fulfillment are available to every adopted person. Yes, that includes you.

On the other side of the pain is the person you've been waiting for. The person who calls out to you from the deepest places inside. You know that voice! It's time to listen to it because you're worthy of freeing that person. You're worthy of becoming all you're meant to be, because you're a hero.

We can do this. Despite it all, we can thrive as adopted people! Finding a way back to a place of harmony inside after loss, rejection, or removal disconnects us from ourselves is our journey back home. It's the courageous innermost walk toward becoming whole. I've discovered that healing the soul and coming home to self is the most transformational reunion an adoptee, or anyone, will ever have.

I never had the chance to reunite with my first father, in the physical sense of the word. After his death, I did meet the brother I never knew I had. We met on a rainy afternoon in Spain, in 2012. Antonio told me that our father spoke of me one month before his passing, saying, "I have a daughter out there somewhere." Although I had been told a very different story all my life, I believe that my father did want to know when I was born because, as I'd discovered, he knew that he had a daughter.

The complexities of life — and the secrets that Juliáno held — had stood in the way of his reaching out to me. Yet, in that moment I connected with my father. He let me know, through Antonio, that he'd carried me within his heart all along.

Several years after that revelation, I spoke with an intuitive on the phone. She knew nothing of my story and was aware only of my first name. As we began our session, she said a man stepped forward in her vision. The intuitive referred to this man as "a Spaniard." This person had an urgent message for me: "I never meant not to be a good man." I knew immediately that this was Juliáno letting me know that he never intended to hurt me. I'd waited for those words all my life, and they finally arrived after my father had left this earth.

It wouldn't have been possible for me to receive these divine messages had I not begun the work of healing the eight adoptee pain points before learning of Juliáno's death. You see, I'd been on my own soul-healing journey. That process of transformational clearing, which comes with a good dose of forgiving, had created an opening for my father to reveal — from a spiritual place — his love for me, along with the sorrow he felt for leaving me.

We tend to think that adoption reunion can look only one way — that it has to be a face-to-face event. That's a disempowering thought, though. It's a limiting belief! I'm here to say that adoptee reunion can be spiritual and divinely guided. I've lived it!

My hope of hopes is that this book will be a source of divine guidance as you begin healing these primary sources of pain — clearing the way for a transformational reunion of self and of spirit, as an adoptee. The exercises and stories, affirmations and awakenings in this book are intended to illuminate the path toward your true north as you reunite with yourself, reconcile with your adoption story, and reframe your life.

You will find the pause symbol —ᴠᴠ— after certain passages throughout this book. This symbol suggests that the moment can serve as a time of adoptee awakening. It's an opportunity for you to sit in stillness and feel your truth lighting up within you. It's also a time when you may want to write your thoughts in your journal. Or you may want to speak your thoughts out loud and release them this way. Whatever feels right for you, please give yourself the gift of acknowledging the feelings and thoughts that come to you. We have to feel the hurt in order to heal the hurt.

I believe that everything you need to heal and move forward in your life is found within you right here and right now. You possess a wellspring of wisdom that has been born of your experiences as an adoptee. It's time to believe in that wisdom. Take these moments of adoptee awakening, and allow yourself to look at the pain points that speak to you. It's the wound calling out for you to go deeper. If the wound is the place where the light enters you, and I believe that it is, then you must go there. You don't have to go there alone, though. I am with you.

I learned the words *Sat Nam* several years ago while in India. The words mean "truth identified." Every time I speak these words, either out loud or in my own quiet moments of stillness, they bring tears to my eyes. My life journey as an adoptee has been a quest to identify my truth and to encounter the power of that truth.

This is my heartfelt prayer for you: may this book illuminate the way toward your truth as you identify what is sacred and real within you and reunite with yourself on the deepest and most profound levels. *Sat Nam.*

CHAPTER ONE

Labeled and Lessened

Feeling Unwelcome in the World

It's 3 p.m. in Scottsdale, Arizona, February 2021. I'm sitting in the tattoo artist's chair. I've never had a tattoo before, so this is new to me. I take a deep breath and close my eyes while the artist, a friendly guy named Joe, places a template of the design I've requested on my right arm. I look down at the two words on my arm and smile. "There she is," I say. "So what does the name mean?" Joe asks. "It's my name before I was adopted, Julié Dawn. I'm an international adoptee. My name was changed to Michelle when my adoption was finalized. I think it's appropriate that my first tattoo is the name of my first me."

"Well, you never forget your first time or your first one." Joe laughs at his own humor and adds, "Does the placement seem good for you?" I chuckle, scan the template, and say, "Julié Dawn looks beautiful. Let's do it." I watch as Joe uses his tattoo pen to begin inking my very first name in a fine, delicate font. I couldn't get his words off my mind: *you never forget your first one.*

Joe was right. I had tried for years to forget my first me, Julié Dawn, but I couldn't. She was a real and present part of me yet someone I felt I had to keep hidden away. I'd been segregated from my first self, and I'd suffered for it. Unsure of who I was and uncomfortable in my own skin, I believed that I was unworthy of love and incapable of greater things. For some reason, I felt safe to share these truths with Joe. I assume this sense of safety was in large part due to the intimacy of him scripting something permanent onto my skin.

I confessed to Joe that I had pushed Julié Dawn into the shadows for a very long time. I didn't believe that she was welcome in the world. After all, she'd been left by her first parents — my first parents. I had never been able to forget my first parents, either.

"Gosh, I feel pretty emotional," I said. "It's kind of an unexpected feeling. Watching you ink the words *Julié Dawn* on my arm is like witnessing her coming back to life. I've done a whole lot of internal work over the years to pull her out of the shadows. For me this moment is like an outer declaration of an inner transformation."

I could see that my words had moved Joe. His eyes were welling up as he replied, "I'm glad that I can help." My attention shifted to a song, "Come Home," by the group OneRepublic, that was playing in the background. The lyrics were sung like an invitation of reunion meant just for Julié Dawn and me.

By the end of the song, Joe was putting the final touches on my tattoo and I felt oddly exhilarated. Julié Dawn was being liberated! She was coming home for all the world to see. There was a time when I didn't believe that I could ever outwardly claim my first me. I could never forget her, Joe was right, but claiming her out loud was a very different thing. I'd been caught up in a tug-of-war of identity. All my life I'd struggled with where to place Julié Dawn. I had felt shame for silencing her and guilt for even thinking of her. I had been angry at myself for fighting against what was true in order to keep everyone else around me happy.

Now the truth was permanently inked on my right arm. I felt empowered by that! I would no longer hide the person I was before adoption, nor would I continue to force that part of me into submission. This tattoo would forever be my reminder that becoming whole requires that I embrace all of me.

As I sit here and write these words, I pause and allow my left index finger to trace the letters of my tattoo. I have butterflies in my stomach because I can feel the intense insecurity that I experienced growing up as a former foster child and international adoptee. I can feel the gut-wrenching sadness and confusion of displacement and removal. I can remember that sense of unexplainable loss.

I know these emotions well. I understand the silencing of voice when, as an adoptee, you're told to just forget about the past and move on. I know how comments like that can make you feel invisible. I've experienced the unfairness firsthand. There was a time when my spirit felt diminished. Today I can look back on these moments without being swallowed up by the callous comments and unjust expectations that once made me feel so small.

I'm proud of myself for that. Yet, I'm most proud that I kept going even when I wanted to quit. I'm proud that I keep going. It's a day-by-day process, a practice. The journey of healing is never linear; it's filled with unexpected detours and setbacks. Through it all, I'm committed to showing up each day and learning more about who I'm here to be.

Here's something I know for sure: I was never made for living as half of who I am. I wasn't made for living only one side of the adoptee journey. There's both shine and shadow found within the adoption experience. I've learned to honor both in order to find my fullest worth along the way.

I've done a lot of inner work to become whole. What has been most healing for me is creating soulful space for accessing an internal wisdom that awaits beyond the wounds of abandonment, rejection, and relinquishment. I've longed to hear the truth of my voice ring out over the once-deafening narrative that I was given before I could even speak. I've learned to trust my voice. I've prayed to find the lost places inside myself. I've learned how to reunite with those places, to come home to myself, and to define on my own terms what home looks like for me.

I've learned to welcome every part of my story, as imperfect as it is, into my life and my work. What I've discovered along the way is that there are miracles in the messiness of life. If you run from the mess, you'll never ignite the brilliant and miraculous light inside you. And the world needs all your light — every single spark. You need all your light, too.

I feel fully ignited in my life today because I became brave enough to look at the messy parts of my story and identify what was keeping me in a place of deep, dark suffering. I showed up for my own healing and, day by day, I built a solid foundation of self-credibility. That self-credibility has built trust within me — showing me that I can overcome the pain points of this adoptee experience and learn to thrive.

Adoptees are crying out to find a way back to themselves and to end the suffering that they've been conditioned to believe they have no power to heal. I know that adoptees can heal their life. I know this because I'm proof, and I have the privilege of witnessing those I coach heal and become more than they ever thought they could be.

As I sit at my desk, I'm surrounded by images of horses and hummingbirds. Tibetan singing bowls sit close to me, and candles are burning bright. My teenage son and daughter, both international adoptees, are upstairs resting in their bedrooms. Our home is peaceful and quiet.

My journey of self-healing has brought me to this place of peace. Finally, there is peace! Writing these words, I remember who I am. I've come home to me. It's been a profound journey of reunion, one that assists me in guiding you along your own journey toward peace, wholeness, and a greater way forward.

A Willingness to Thrive

Let me take you back a few years, to 2010. That's when I held my daughter for the first time. She was ten months old. I remember the slow-moving moments spent waiting for her to be brought to me from inside the orphanage. I recall passing the time by counting raindrops that were dripping off a metal roof and creating puddles at my feet. It was Ethiopia's rainy season.

I was seriously jet-lagged after only arriving in Addis Ababa a short two hours earlier. The flight had been a twenty-hour journey that took me through Paris, Dubai, and on to Ethiopia's capital. I remember how the plane banked to the south and dipped its wings toward the fertile land below. I pressed my forehead tightly against the window and peeked through the clouds. They parted so gracefully, revealing a dense covering of eucalyptus trees that rolled off the slopes of Mount Entoto.

I spotted little round huts in the distance. Wisps of smoke emerged from the thatched roofs and mingled with the mist hanging in the air. The scenes flew swiftly by, and I knew my life would be forever changed once the plane landed.

I cleared customs with my daughter's daddy, Jeff. We received our visas, making our way through the airport and toward baggage claim. I passed mothers carrying their children in their arms. Some were dressed in Western clothes, while others were cloaked in burqas. I smiled at them, not knowing if they were smiling back. I felt somehow exposed in their presence, and so I reached into my handbag for a scarf, wrapping it around my head as I waited for my luggage.

It wasn't long before our suitcases were in hand and we connected with the driver who was waiting for us outside the arrival terminal. Abal set out for the hotel and raced along the washed-out roads, narrowly avoiding the large puddles and potholes left in the wake of heavy rains. There were young boys herding goats in the streets as the traffic around them grew more and more congested. I marveled at their ability to seamlessly navigate the goats through what appeared, to me, as mayhem.

Abal pulled up to the hotel as security guards met his car. They checked under, inside, and around the vehicle to ensure that there were no explosive devices. Once we were okayed to proceed forward, Jeff and I checked in and were shown to our room.

We hadn't settled in for much more than five minutes before the phone rang, alerting us that our attorney was waiting in the lobby. We hurried downstairs to greet Abebe. He was a big man, warm in personality, and had updated news to share. Abebe told us that we'd been given permission to meet our daughter that afternoon. If we wanted to take the opportunity, we'd need to leave immediately.

Our smiles signaled to Abebe that we were absolutely willing to leave at that moment. Jeff and I climbed into a waiting van and were on our way to see our baby girl. I sat silently as we headed out of the city, thinking about all the events that had conspired over the past fourteen months to bring us to this moment. The many random conversations with strangers who mentioned Ethiopia in passing, and my own intuitive voice that urged me to take note of these conversations. They were signs, I believed, like little pebbles along a path moving me closer and closer to my daughter. Sitting in that van, in Addis Ababa, it hit me that the entire process had seemed like forever yet also like the blink of an eye.

I didn't view adoption as saving a child. God knows, I'm no savior. I hadn't chosen this path of adopting in order to fill some empty part of myself. My own experience as an adoptee had shown me the mental and emotional stress that is created when a parent puts that kind of responsibility on their child. Perhaps I knew that I could give to my two internationally adopted children what I did not receive growing up. I could love and accept them as they are and let them be who they are here to be. I could embrace every part of their story and identity and openly honor their first families and first countries. I could acknowledge the loss they experienced because I know it's real. I could say, I understand.

Twenty minutes into our drive, Abebe turned down a narrow dirt road. I recognized it from the videos I had watched on YouTube, posted by other families who had traveled this same path. "We are so close," I said to Jeff. A strange sense of awareness welled up in me. I saw an old sign, marking the name of the orphanage, and began to cry. Abebe stopped and spoke a few words in Amharic to the guard. Slowly, the gate that stood between us and our baby girl swung open.

We quickly stepped out of Abebe's van, after it came to a halt, and hurried toward an area of shelter from the rain. A little boy pedaled up to us on a rusty bike. "Who are you?" he asked. "I'm Michelle. I'm here to meet my daughter. Who are you?" "I'm eight!" The boy held up eight fingers, laughed, and scurried away through a muddy mixture of rain and dirt. He was one of a hundred orphaned children living inside the compound.

Jeff and I were escorted into a waiting room with walls the color of creamed coffee. The rugs were frayed and the couches were worn. I slipped out of my raincoat, took off my sweater, and warmed my skin — preparing for the moment when I would hold my baby.

Jeff was becoming impatient, and so we stepped out onto the covered porch and began counting raindrops, one by one, calming our quickening heartbeats. Suddenly, I saw a woman walking toward us. She was holding a tiny human in her arms. As they approached, I realized that this little bundle of life was the daughter I'd come to bring home. Without a word, the woman — my daughter's caregiver — placed her into my arms.

"Hello," I whispered through my tears. "Let's get you inside and out of the damp." Jeff and I stepped back into the family area of the orphanage. We pulled a tiny music box from our bag — a gift

Jeff had purchased in Paris — and began playing a lullaby for our little one. As we settled our baby girl, the orphanage director slipped through a side door.

Naomi carried a thin file in her hands, containing the only information they'd gathered about our baby. "Your daughter was found all alone, by locals in southern Ethiopia, in an area called Arba Minch. A police officer came to retrieve her and gave her a name, Tiblet."

"What does the name mean?" I asked.

"The translation is Let Her Be Greater," Naomi explained.

It seemed that a stranger had given my daughter a name that carried with it the wish that she would become more than her circumstances. The meaning of my baby's name felt like a divine message — a crying out to the heavens that she would emerge from the shattered pieces of her story and step fully into the promise of her worth.

I gazed down at our precious little girl as I held her in my arms. It was clear that she was sick and frail. She didn't smell of baby powder and scented lotion, but to me she was the sweetest little human I'd ever seen. I witnessed, like scenes from a film flashing before my eyes, all the promise, potential, and power she possessed — the power to become everything she would ever dream of becoming. I saw her worth. In an instant I saw it. I could see all this in my daughter, but I couldn't see the same value in myself.

Why was it so hard for me to catch a glimpse of my own potential and worth? This was a question I knew I had to answer for myself. It was a question that I had long been avoiding. At that moment, however, I shifted my full attention onto the child in my arms, who had now lowered her head onto my shoulder and nodded off to sleep. *Let her be greater.* I whispered the words of my daughter's name into her soft and tender ear.

As the days passed, it became more and more evident that my

daughter was riddled with illness. She was battling giardia caused by the unclean water she'd been exposed to. This severe parasite infection was robbing her of nutrition and causing bouts of explosive diarrhea. Her tiny body was suffering from malnourishment.

I inquired about seeking medical attention for her while on the ground in Ethiopia but was told that her unsettled digestion was likely due to the newness of her environment and the changes that had recently occurred. My motherly instinct knew different, but I continued to treat her symptoms, as best as I could, while in Addis Ababa.

Jeff and I spent ten days in Ethiopia with our daughter as we finalized her adoption and prepared for the flight back to America. I recall the kindness shown by the many people we met along the way, from the hand-over-heart gesture we were so often greeted with — along with the word *selam*, which means "peace" — to the support of the flight attendants on Emirates Airways on the flight from Dubai to New York, as I changed countless diapers and cared for my ailing child. Through it all, I was reminded of the goodness of people around the world. This offered me so much hope.

When we arrived home, the US doctors gave my daughter a diagnosis of *failure to thrive*. This diagnosis struck me on the deepest levels. I was determined to help my baby heal. At the same time, as I stared into my girl's watery eyes, I saw a reflection of my own condition. In that moment, I realized that this was the exact diagnosis I'd given myself as a foster child and adoptee. I'd been living this self-diagnosis: expecting life to fail me.

All my life, I had felt weakened by my adoption story. Daily, since I was a child, I had asked myself why my first parents left me. I felt as if I'd failed them somehow, but I didn't have a clue as to what I'd done. It was maddening.

Why would my parents leave unless something was wrong with me? Something must have been terribly flawed about me to make them turn away. It was the only logical answer that came to me. I had failed them. I was a failure. And failures don't thrive.

The wound of abandonment was deep and raw. I was existing from this place of failure and in a constant mode of fight-flight-freeze-fawn, all of which are trauma responses in stressful situations. Survivors of trauma often live in one or more of these modes. The fight response is the body's way of aggressively facing a perceived threat. The flight response is the body's way of urging you to flee from danger. The freeze response is the body's inability to act against a threat. The fawn response is the body's attempt to please someone in order to stay safe and avoid conflict.

I smelled danger all around me. If my earliest parental bonds had failed, then how could anything else in my life succeed? I had anticipated, for as long as I could remember, nothing more than a failure-to-thrive outcome in all areas of my life. Now, staring into the eyes of my daughter, I knew this had to change.

I didn't want to be an example of failure for my daughter. I was tired of seeing a failure when I looked in the mirror. I couldn't bear the thought of another second spent scrambling to merely survive, or another minute spent hustling to prove a sense of value that I wasn't even convinced I possessed. As I worked to heal my baby's tiny body, I also began the work of healing myself — emotionally and mentally — of the dis-ease I'd been living with as an adoptee.

I'd never felt comfortable in my own skin. Since my earliest moments, I had felt unwelcome in the world, an overwhelming sensation. I saw myself as discarded by my first parents and lessened by their actions and choices. The early wound of abandonment had caused me to feel irrelevant in my adult life.

It was as if my parents' attitudes about my conception could never be erased from my memory. I had entered the world as their shameful mistake. I was their guarded secret. It's how I'd been living my life: labeled by my circumstances, devalued and dehumanized as an unwanted child. The chatter in my mind was nagging at me, day and night, and reminding me that I was unwelcome in the world. It was a noise that seemed impossible to quiet.

Our thoughts become the words we use with ourselves. Those words narrate our beliefs, and our beliefs become the reality that we live in. How did I sense, as an adoptee, that survival was my only option? I was exhausted from being constantly on guard. When did I first start believing that I was unwanted — unwelcome — in the world? I had felt this from as early as I could remember. Is it possible that I somehow had received this messaging before I was even born?

Our Stories Begin in the Womb

I have a strong belief that, within the womb, babies feel what their mother feels. They hear the words spoken by their mother. They soak up her energy. They develop a sense of touch. They draw powerful life force from the emotional cradling as they experience their mother's emotions, bond, and grow in those beginning moments of life. As one mother wrote to me, "I'm that first mother/birth mother, and I know that my daughter felt everything!"

For adoptees these primal, early moments can be clouded by an awareness that something isn't right. We sense our mother's struggle: Will she keep us or let us go? We fight, on a cellular level, for the bond with our mother to continue. We fear the bond's fragility and await its failure.

This belief was scientifically confirmed to me during a conference in November 2020. I sat in on a presentation by author and international speaker Bruce Lipton, who wrote the book *The Biology of Belief: Unleashing the Power of Consciousness, Matter & Miracles*. Lipton writes: "Once the child is conceived, an impressive body of research is documenting how important parents' attitudes are in the development of the fetus."

Lipton goes on to quote authors Thomas R. Verny and Pamela

Weintraub from their book *Pre-parenting: Nurturing Your Child from Conception*: "In fact, the great weight of the scientific evidence that has emerged over the last decade demands that we reevaluate the mental and emotional abilities of unborn children. Awake or asleep, the studies show, they are constantly tuned in to their mother's every action, thought, and feeling. From the moment of conception, the experience in the womb shapes the brain and lays the groundwork for personality, emotional temperament, and the power of higher thought."

Lipton explains, "If the mother is under stress, she activates her HPA axis, which provides fight-or-flight responses in a threatening environment." The HPA axis plays a pivotal role in regulating the synthesis and release of hormones associated with the central nervous system, including cortisol, which is a major stress hormone with widespread effects throughout the body.

Lipton continues, "Stress hormones prepare the body to engage in a protection response. Once these maternal signals enter the fetal blood stream, they affect the same target tissues and organs in the fetus as they did in the mother."

A 2013 article from the Post Institute stated, "Scientific research now reveals that as early as the second trimester, the human fetus is capable of auditory processing and in fact, is capable of processing rejection in utero."

Science continues to prove that an unborn child can be programmed with the fear of rejection and a fight-flight-freeze-fawn response from before they are delivered into the world. Based on this body of scientific evidence, it is safe to say that the unborn adoptee can feel what their mother feels, can experience what their mother experiences, and can hear what their mother is hearing and saying. If their mother is under stress, then so, too, is the adoptee. They've been wired with a protective response from before they were even born.

Lipton goes on, "The lesson for adoptive parents is that they should not pretend their children's lives began when they came into their new surroundings. Their children may have already been programmed with a belief that they are unwanted or unlovable. If more fortunate, they may have, at some crucial age in their development, received positive, life-affirming messages from their caretakers. If adoptive parents are not aware of pre- and perinatal programming, they may not deal realistically with post-adoption issues."

I'm not a scientist, but in my opinion the above evidence goes a long way in supporting what many adoptees have felt and are just beginning to express out loud: *I was there.* These three words have been perhaps the most unspoken and understated words in the adoptee community.

It's time for this truth to be spoken within the wider adoption conversation. The belief that adoptees didn't feel the bonds created within their first mother's womb, or that they didn't sense their hearts breaking at the severing of those bonds, is highly detrimental. And science is proving that this belief is false. As I sat and listened to Dr. Lipton's presentation, it became crystal clear that adoptees were *there* for it all. They just haven't been given the space to openly explore and express what that means for them.

Adoptees Didn't Enter the World as Blank Slates

It's vital that we as adoptees come to realize that we didn't enter the world as "blank slates." We were programmed during the months spent inside our mother's womb. We need to recognize this programming and work to change it — to reprogram the programming — if its messaging does not serve our highest good.

When we recognize that in utero programming is real, we are better equipped to deal with postadoption issues, whether they be in the lives of children and youth who are adopted or in the lives of adult adoptees still struggling with their own early programming. There is hope! And growth and transformation, for any human, are best nurtured within a space of love.

In her book *Happy Days: The Guided Path from Trauma to Profound Freedom and Inner Peace*, Gabrielle Bernstein writes, "Deep within all of us is a loving truth, but we've built up walls against it. Undoing the patterns, thought forms, and programming we were brought up to believe is what's required to return to the truth of who we are. There's nothing 'out there' that can give us that love; it's already within us."

I truly appreciate this quote. It gives me a whole lot of encouragement, and I hope it encourages you, too. Here's the really good news: we, as adoptees, are not stuck with the earliest programming that doesn't serve us in the here and now. We can rewire that programming, undo the harmful patterns, choose new thoughts, and change our life.

I'm here to remind you that you deserve to live fully plugged in to the energy of who you really are. You deserve to do that from the deepest place inside your soul. Every adoptee deserves, once and for all, to rid themselves of the negative labels and limiting beliefs that have lessened them. Adoptees can give themselves permission to step back into their truth, reclaiming all that was once relinquished within.

—◊◊◊—

ADOPTEE AWAKENING: *Adoptee stories begin in the womb. Adoptees have a perceived sense of the world and their place in it before they even take their first breath. Adoptees enter the world with a great deal of information.*

Relinquishment of Self

Fifteen years ago, some three years before I adopted my daughter, I stood in my first mother's bedroom. I was in England and had joined her for lunch and conversation. Late that afternoon, as I was preparing to leave, she grabbed my hand and said, "Please come into my bedroom with me. I have something to show you."

I had no clue as to what my mum was about to reveal to me, but I could sense that it was of great urgency to her. I had reunited with my mum while in my teens and had visited her fairly frequently over the years. I couldn't imagine what could be so pressing now after all this time.

I still remember, almost word for word, the initial search letter that I wrote to anyone who would be willing to read it. The letter was addressed to the Royal Air Force, where my first mother's husband had served. I was a gutsy teenage girl, nearly sixteen, searching for her mother and was unsure if a stranger opening my letter would even care, yet I implored them to read my words through to the end. I wrote that I needed an angel to help me find my mum and hoped that they would be that angel. I mailed that letter from where I was in America and several weeks later, I received a reply from my first mother's husband. He wanted proof that I was who I said I was. He said that my first mother had suffered greatly after letting me go, and he didn't want to risk her suffering again. I sent proof back in the form of paperwork with my original name of Julié Dawn on it.

Once my mother's husband received my letter and the paperwork confirming my identity, both were shared with her. A few short weeks after that, I stood in the crowded Heathrow Airport in London. I had flown back to my birth country, alone, to begin the journey of reconciliation with my first mother and with myself. My heart was beating out of my chest. As the crowd parted in the arrival terminal, I saw my mum standing there in a lilac-colored dress. My initial emotion was one of anger for all the years spent apart from her. I had suffered, too. Yet, as I moved closer to my mum, the anger faded away and I melted into her arms as we shared a long and overdue embrace.

Now, as an adult, I followed my mum into her bedroom as she closed the door behind us. I stood by her bed as she opened a shallow drawer and sifted through its contents. Looking around my first mother's room, it seemed as if I had stepped into her childhood past. There were stuffed animals everywhere of all shapes and sizes.

An awareness shot through me like a bolt of lightning that my mum was a wounded little girl. I'd never felt this overwhelming sensation before while in her presence. It filled me with sorrow to think that perhaps she'd never been able to do the kind of deep healing work that I'd started for myself.

Mum turned around and walked toward me with a small brown envelope in her hand. She said, "I've been holding on to this for years and years. I want you to have it now." I took the envelope from her hand and slowly opened it. I pulled out the folded piece of paper and saw that it was our original letter of relinquishment from so long ago.

I said softly, "I have the copy of this letter but I've never seen the original. Somehow, Mum, this hits me differently. It makes me so sad. It's as if I can feel your hand pressing against the paper as you signed your name here, giving up your rights to raise me."

I began to weep uncontrollably. Mum began to weep, too. She said, "I never wanted to let you go. I agonized over the decision, but I had no choice, or at least I didn't believe that I had any choice. I need you to know that I didn't want to let you go."

Mum fell into my arms and I embraced her. I rocked her like a little baby and said, "I have missed Julié Dawn all my life, Mum. I haven't known how to grieve her or where to place her. I haven't known how to grieve you or where to place you, either. It's been so hard. As hard as it's been for me, I know that it's been hard for you, too. We both lost so much. I'm truly glad that you chose to bring me into this world, but my entire life has been spent trying to come back to something inside myself that I feel removed from. I think that thing is self-love, Mum. I think that when you relinquished your rights to raise me, I may have unknowingly relinquished my rights to love me."

Mum and I cried for the longest time. There was so much grief to let out — so much grief still to process. Looking back on my first mother's relinquishment letter, I see that it represented more than her parental rights being given up. It also represented my relinquishment of any sense of inner value, self-love, and worth.

Earlier I shared that I asked myself this question while in Ethiopia: *Why was it so hard to catch a glimpse of my own potential and worth?* I think the answer is this: I had lost a sense of self-value when I lost my mum. I didn't believe that I was worthy of being valued by myself or anyone else around me. I didn't believe that I was welcome in the world. It's no wonder life seemed so frightening and relationships so fragile.

I didn't know at the time that the hard things that happened to me were not a reflection of my inner worth. The decisions made around me could not define me unless I allowed them to. Adoptees often carry the weight of those outside decisions on their shoulders. Here's the truth: the baggage of others was never ours to carry. This was a major awakening in my life. I had been carrying the baggage of secrecy, judgment, guilt, and shame — all related to the circumstances of my early life and relinquishment. Ultimately, I needed to put those heavy burdens down and let them go. They were never mine to own.

———ɱɱ———

ADOPTEE AWAKENING: *Others' baggage was never the adoptee's burden to carry.*

Yet we can carry the baggage of others for a really long time, can't we? As adopted people, we carry so much of that weight. The weight of abandonment, fear of rejection, feelings of disconnection, shame and blame, guilt and remorse.

Their baggage becomes ours. Our minds whisper, *They left, and so we aren't worthy of being cherished and loved. We are their secret, and so we have to live small and silence our truth. We were someone's gift, and so we must always be perfect so that they don't send us away, too. We're expected to be grateful, and so we can never openly grieve.* The whispers go on and on ...

REFLECTION EXERCISE
Putting Down the Baggage

Let me ask you this question: *As an adoptee, what baggage are you carrying that does not belong to you?* This baggage could be a limiting belief you've always carried or beliefs that came up for you while reviewing the Dickens Process in the introduction.

Take a moment and go deep. Write down anything that comes to you. There are no right or wrong answers, only your truth to be explored. Once you're through this part of the exercise, reflect on what carrying this baggage has cost you and those you care about. See it. Hear it. Feel it. How might this baggage be hindering you and those you love from living more joyfully today? How might it be stifling your sense of self-worth in the here and now? See it. Hear it. Feel it. Who will be suffering the most one year, three years, five years, or ten years from now if you continue to claim this baggage? What will your life look like? What will the lives of those you care about look like? See it. Hear it. Feel it.

Now close your eyes and envision yourself putting that baggage down. Once and for all you're letting it go. Bless it for showing you what you no longer want in your life so that you can redirect yourself toward what you do want. See what you want. Hear the sounds of your desires. Feel the energy of no longer being burdened by the baggage.

Write down what you do want. Get clear! What new beliefs are you ready to pick up? Where do you want to be one year, three years, five years, or ten years from now? Who will be with you? What will you be doing? How will you feel? Let yourself go there. Write everything down in as much detail as you possibly can. It's vital to identify where we are, as adoptees, and where we want to be. In other words, this is the current location and the ultimate destination of our vision work. In between your current location and your ultimate destination is the gap. The gap is what's keeping you from realizing and arriving at the destination you hold in your heart.

For me, once I worked through the above process, I realized that reconnecting to a place of self-worth and potential was my journey. I wanted to feel fully alive and ignited by an unstoppable sense of self-worth and potential. The gap, for me, was a disconnection between my mind/body/spirit that was keeping me from my desired destination. I had unplugged from feeling anything, at some point in my life, and it took the shine out of me. I had become numb in order to avoid the hurt ... and I knew it.

The Housing of Our Hurt

Feelings of unworthiness are often buried deep. Several years ago I attended a healing session with a Maori healer from New Zealand, who said, "Pain is housed in the bones. If we don't do the work of going deep to find it, it causes a state of dis-ease within us."

So very often, during one-on-one coaching sessions or when I'm speaking to a group of adoptees, they share this: *I feel unworthy and I don't know what that means. I just know I feel unsettled within myself.* I believe these adoptees are describing this sense of dis-ease the Maori healer spoke of. They feel unworthy of love. This mental and emotional block hinders adoptees from realizing so many of their hopes and dreams.

If adoptees feel unworthy of love — the profoundest of human needs — then how can they realize meaningful success, advance their career goals, enjoy authentic relationships both romantic and platonic, and obtain abundant health and wholeness?

—⟋⟍—

ADOPTEE AWAKENING: *Behind all the fears and blocks that keep adoptees from connecting to a profound sense of love is the limiting belief that they are unwelcome in the world.*

Sit with the above awakening thought for a moment. As I stated in the introduction, my first mother contemplated aborting me on three different occasions. I shared that she spent a great deal of time meeting with psychiatrists as she evaluated her options and searched for the answer as to whether an abortion was the right decision for her. I stated that I spent my unborn days treading the waters of life inside my mother's womb. If you believe, as I do, that what scientific evidence says is true, then I experienced the stress my mother was under and the panic she felt as she struggled with her difficult decision — the very real and human decision — of whether to abort me or bring me to term.

I hold an immense amount of gratitude that my mother was presented with choice during a most challenging time in her life, and that her choice was ultimately to give birth to me. I reiterate this part of our story, void of any judgment, because it's critical to understand that the womb, for the unborn adopted child, can feel like the very point where the separation from their mother begins.

This condition of separation, of loss, can signal to the adoptee that they are unwelcome. The feeling follows them into the world and shapes how they see themselves. It's imperative that adoptees are offered the safe space needed to openly give voice to this sense of feeling unwelcome. If a safe space isn't created, then adoptees may silently translate their feelings as concrete evidence that they are not accepted, desired, or welcomed into every aspect of their life. The primal voice within that speaks of early loss can be louder than any inherent truth of who they are or what they're here to contribute.

If adoptees have been wired with a protection response — a fight-flight-freeze-fawn existence — from within the womb, it is essential that they are supported and guided to rewire that programming, put the baggage down, and fully believe and claim, *"I am safe. I am loved. I am wanted. I am welcome in my life."*

Penelope and Her Struggle with Feeling Unwelcome

During one of our coaching sessions, Penelope, an adult transracial adoptee, shared her intense fear of entering social situations. This fear had impaired her ability to experience a sense of real connection in her life and in her relationships.

"I feel anxious and fearful whenever I have to engage with people and speak with them. It's like I'm already predicting, in my head, that they will want me to leave — that I won't be welcome within their circle. I'm afraid I'll be shunned and sent away." Penelope, a mother of four, went on to share that she is even convinced that she's an embarrassment to her family and that they, too, will want her to leave at some point.

When I asked Penelope to rank each of the eight pain points of adoption from 1 to 10, 1 being the pain is hardly ever felt and 10 being the pain is felt most or all the time, she ranked the pain of feeling unwelcome in the world as a 10.

"It's the first thing I think about when I wake up. The thought of being unwelcome follows me throughout my day. It's in the front of my mind, no matter what I do. It's the last thing I think about before I go to sleep. I don't know how to change it," she said through her tears.

This pain point, for Penelope, of being unwelcome in the world had become permanent, pervasive, and personal. Permanent in that she felt the problem would never go away. Pervasive in that she felt the problem dominated her so much that it was her life. And personal in that the problem, in her mind, had become who she was.

Penelope felt pushed to the outskirts of living, as if she was hanging on the fringes and awaiting it all to fail. "I live my life expecting that everything will fall apart at any given time," she said.

As we went deeper into the root cause of Penelope's pain, she shared that she'd always felt unwanted and unaccepted by her first mother. "Why else would she have left me? She didn't want me. She didn't accept me. I think I entered the world feeling this way — like I had a sense of being unwelcome before I was even born. How can I ever see myself as welcomed by anyone if my own mother turned away from me?"

"Have you ever welcomed yourself into your life, Penelope?" I asked.

"What do you mean?"

I explained that she was expressing a fear of others not welcoming her but that she'd never offered herself the welcoming that she longed for from others. As adoptees, being truly embraced and welcomed into our lives starts with us. We need to be able to embrace and welcome ourselves into our life and into our vision for our life. Change begins within. It begins with a deep and soulful invitation to honor ourselves and welcome ourselves into the world as adoptees. We can absolutely invite ourselves back into life and into the fullness of living.

The pain of feeling unwelcome in the world is real, on some level, for most adoptees. It's a valid hurt that needs to be talked about. If it's avoided, the discomfort — the dis-ease — can grow and follow an adoptee into every nook and cranny of their life.

Even special life events can be shadowed by this feeling of being unwelcome. It's why the hardest day on the adoptee's calendar is often their birthday. It's the day that reminds many adoptees not of their birth but of their loss.

—ഝ—

ADOPTEE AWAKENING: *Change begins within.*

Deanna Dreaded Her Birthday

When my coaching client Deanna first came to me, she was struggling with the thought of her approaching birthday. "Michelle, I'm dreading my birthday. It's coming up in two weeks and I want to crawl under a blanket and sleep until it's over!" Deanna's voice was trembling as we began our session.

Deanna described her impending birthday using strong words that signaled the intensity of the pain she was experiencing — a 9.5 on the scale — as she struggled with feeling unwelcome in the world. She shared that she was exhausted from years of pretending to be enthusiastic about her birthday when, in truth, it made her incredibly sad.

Deanna's adoption was an open one. As a kid, she vividly remembers a visit from her bio mother just a few days before her eighth birthday. The two sat down on Deanna's back porch, and that's when her bio mother confided in Deanna that the day she was born was a "terrible, terrible day."

Deanna didn't know exactly what her bio mother meant by those words, but she remembers feeling ashamed that she was ever born. Those words stayed with Deanna, seeding the belief that she was unwelcome in the world.

I understood Deanna's pain. My first mother had said something very similar when I was a teenager visiting her in England. We'd gone on a daylong train trip and were somewhere between her village and the larger city of Lincoln, in Lincolnshire. I took the opportunity, while sitting knee to knee with my mum, to inquire about the day I was born. She said, while staring out the train window, "It was the worst day of my life."

I felt like I'd had all the wind knocked out of me. I caught my breath and held back my tears. The voice inside my head was saying, *Don't let her see you cry.* I had taken my mum's words straight to my heart. The day of my birth was her worst day. I was convinced of it. Why would she say it if it wasn't?

As a result I ignored and avoided my birthday, as much as possible, from that day forward. What I heard on the train was that I was the cause of my mother's worst day. I was the cause! It solidified my belief that I had failed her. The voice in my head was loud. It told me that, from the earliest moments of my existence, I was a failure.

It took years of coaching, healing, and reframing for me to understand what I now know to be true: my first mother's statement wasn't about me personally. The day of my birth wasn't her worst day because she had me — it was her worst day because she knew she'd have to leave me. She felt that struggle while she carried me in her womb. It was our shared struggle. We weren't mother and child while I was inside her; we were mother/child. We were one.

As I coached Penelope and Deanna through reframing the pain of feeling unwelcome in the world, the process reminded me of healing my former self: an adoptee who once struggled with the emotions experienced in her mother's womb. Like me and so many other adoptees, Penelope and Deanna *were there.* They experienced in the womb what their mothers experienced in the world. So much unspoken pain lingered for both women.

It's safe to say that this pain point, feeling unwelcome, had become both Penelope's and Deanna's life and identity. Remember what I shared about the three *ps* of Penelope's pain? For both women, this pain point had become permanent, pervasive, and personal. This was Penelope's focused thought inside both family and social settings. It was Deanna's focused thought every year as her birthday approached.

Where Focus Goes, Energy Flows

There's a coaching mantra that I adhere to in my life and in my work. It's the same mantra that I use to awaken my coaching clients to the importance of focus: *Where focus goes, energy flows.* Our focus creates our experience; it shapes our reality.

This mantra also links back to Bruce Lipton's theory in his book *The Biology of Belief.* There is a connection between mind and matter! What we hold in our mind — along with the thoughts and beliefs we focus on — impacts the quality of our health and our emotions and our ability to thrive.

I focused, for so long, on being my first parents' shameful secret and the cause of my first mother's worst day that the energy of these thoughts followed me everywhere I went. I didn't know, for a very long time, that I could change my focus and create a new and empowering energy flow. You possess the same ability — all adoptees do.

Unleashing our power as adoptees starts with our willingness to find a whole new way to focus and to end any self-labeling of being unwelcome or unwanted people. We must be willing to be willing as we step into this transformational journey! As adoptees we are highly capable of moving beyond the limiting programming that has lessened us — some of that programming created during our earliest experiences in the womb. We can embrace ourselves back into the world and begin the lives we're destined for.

What if, as an adoptee, you could connect back to that womb energy from so long ago and create a new energy flow? What if you could birth yourself anew by changing that energy from a limiting sense of being unwelcome in the world to the limitless truth that you are welcome — wanted and needed — in this life you've been given? It's the work I did with Penelope and Deanna, and it transformed the way they see themselves and their potential.

REFRAMING EXERCISE
Welcome to the World Invitation

First, rank pain point number 1, the pain of feeling unwelcome in the world, on a scale from 1 to 10, 1 being the pain is hardly ever felt and 10 being the pain is felt most or all the time. Be honest with yourself. There is no judgment. No shame. *Only love.*

Even if this pain point ranks close to a 1 on your scale, I urge you to try this reframing exercise. Discoveries await you here. There is always something to learn. Note that this exercise is your personal invitation to leave behind any unwelcoming thoughts and step into the fullest embrace of living. Remember, all meaningful relationships begin with a welcome. The relationship with yourself must, too.

The following directives are the steps to reframe this point of pain – transform it into a point of light – and welcome yourself into your life. Please find a quiet space for this exercise. Bring a pencil or pen and some paper with you. Get comfortable, and then take three deep breaths in and release those breaths through long, soulful exhales. Drop down into your heart space – the place where truth and clarity reside.

Your heart beats a hundred thousand times a day. You don't even have to think about it. Your heart beats for you. It's a gift!

Trust your heart as you move through this reframing exercise. From your heart space, move forward with the following steps.

Step 1: Write Your Own Welcome to the World Invitation

- What would your invitation say? What compassionate words of welcome come to you?
- How would you celebrate yourself and all the values and attributes that you bring into this world?
- What would you offer yourself as a welcoming gift? What might this gesture of expression be?
- Where would your welcoming celebration take place? Describe that in as much detail as possible.
- You're the guest of honor, so don't be shy. Go all out and create the invitation of your dreams. Your invitation can be anything and everything you want it to be.

Step 2: Read Your Invitation Out Loud

- From your heart space, read your invitation aloud. You can even read it while looking into the mirror — seeing yourself and witnessing your words.
- Be open to receiving every single word of welcome that you have written.
- Take in your truth. Again, no judgment. Only love.

Step 3: Step Fully into Your Invitation

- Close your eyes once more, and take in another deep and soulful breath. Let that breath gently flow from you with a loving exhale.
- See yourself inside the vision you've created through the words of your invitation.

- Feel the enormous welcoming embrace of your soul. How does it feel? Wrap your arms around yourself and stay with that embrace for as long as you want.
- Let that feeling cover you, let it fall all over you, like confetti from the sky.
- What color is the confetti? See it. Touch it. Delight in it. Be in the moment.
- Who is there celebrating with you? It's okay if you are the only one present. But if someone else is there, see them. See the expression on their face.
- What would you say to your guest or guests? What wisdom would you offer as you lead this welcoming of self?
- Welcome every part of you into every part of your life. Let your words of welcome fill your heart space and guide you from this moment forward. Allow these welcoming words to be the new energy greeting you in all that you do. If ever you feel yourself slipping back into limiting thought, tap yourself on the top of the head and drop back into your heart space. Place your hands over your heart. Breathe into your heart. Envision your special invitation of welcome. These simple steps will bring you back to knowing just how welcome you are in your life. The heart doesn't lie.

As a symbolic gesture of this welcoming, light a candle in your honor. Let the candle's flame remind you of the light you possess within and the renewed hope that this light represents. The light around us is great, but the light within us is greater. Believe in your luminous eternal flame.

As I moved both Penelope and Deanna through this reframing exercise, something miraculous happened for both women: through their visualizations, these adoptees eased the intensity of their feelings of being unwelcome in the world. Their pain points were transformed into points of light. Penelope said, "I no longer feel an overwhelming energy of being unwelcome in my life. I've welcomed myself into living, and it's changed how I enter a room — no matter who is in that room! I feel like I've taken back a power that I had misplaced for years. My pain point has been greatly reduced from a 10 to a 4. I will keep coming back to this exercise. The reframing is powerful!"

Deanna now realizes that the "terrible, terrible day" her bio mother spoke of was not caused by her. "It was a terrible day because my bio mother knew she would have to let me go. When I was in my visualization, I saw the compassion on her face. The day of my birth was a loving day. A hard one, for sure, but love was there. I don't dread or hate my birthday anymore. The pain point has eased. I have the power to control what I focus on, and I focus on celebrating my life — not running from it."

—⚏—

ADOPTEE AWAKENING: *Adoptees are safe to initiate the change they deserve and desire. They are capable of transforming the womb energy that does not support them in the world. Adoptees can begin this energy transformation through a personal invitation of welcome.*

In the next chapter, we'll do the transformational work of realizing reclamation. It's the reintroduction to your earliest self that follows the Welcome to the World Invitation that you just so bravely moved through.

Adoptee Affirmation

I welcome every part of me into every part of my life!
I am safe to know myself, to love myself, and to illuminate
the truth of who I am and why I'm here.

Chapter Two

Realizing Reclamation

Reconnecting a Bond of Communication with the Adoptee's First Me

M any adoptees often suppress what they know to be real for them and struggle with how to explore or even delight in what feels innately theirs. They harbor an underlying fear that others will feel threatened if they learn of the adoptee's true feelings. Many adoptees also fear that love will be withdrawn from them if they make their hidden thoughts known. Suppressing what is real severs not only an external bond of communication but an internal bond as well. Adoptees become more and more distanced from their first me as they practice concealment in order to make the world around them feel safe.

As a kid, before I had reunited with my first mother, Margaret, I traveled to England with my adoptive parents. It was our first trip back to the United Kingdom since my adoption. It was also a trip of concealment. I remember consciously suppressing any joy that I felt over being back in my birth country. I would tell my parents daily, "I like America better." I did this because I knew how happy and relieved it made them feel to hear those words, as if my comments were validation that they'd done the right thing by adopting me.

Making my parents feel better only served to make me feel worse. I had learned, early on, the art of pleasing them for the sake of my own sense of self-preservation and survival. This behavior pattern always left me feeling like a fraud. (Pleasing others over pleasing the self is a topic we'll discuss more in chapter 8.) I do want to say here that people-pleasing — which often begins in the form of parent pleasing — is a common pain point that I guide adoptees in working through. This behavior falls under the trauma response of fawning, one that finds an adoptee prioritizing others over self in an effort to diffuse conflict and receive approval.

Adoptees often find themselves disconnecting from their own wants and needs in order to find a sense of inclusion, acceptance, and love from others. I so deeply feared rejection by my adoptive parents that I felt forced to go underground with the feelings and observations that were real for me as an adoptee, on that first trip back to England and also in my daily life.

The more I disconnected from my true feelings, the more I disconnected from my first me, Julié Dawn, along with the hopes and dreams that she once carried in her heart. I felt far removed from that girl, and I didn't know how to get back to her. I told myself that she didn't matter anymore. Everything and everyone in my adopted world suggested that I should leave the past behind and just move on. And so I worked to erase any memory of my earliest me. I shut down my feelings because it seemed safer not to feel. I neglected my needs. I ignored myself.

—οοο—

ADOPTEE AWAKENING: *Ignoring real needs and disregarding true feelings will only result in the adoptee's abandonment of self, a form of rejection that no adoptee should ever have to experience.*

Abandoning what is real in the adoptee's heart and soul in order to find an external sense of inclusion and acceptance will never bring them the sense of authentic belonging that they may be aching for. Real belonging begins with reclaiming what is true within. Adoptees can offer themselves the most meaningful form of inclusion through reclaiming their first me and reconnecting to the bonds of communication that await them inside this sacred space.

Many of the adult adoptees that I coach today make comments suggesting they've become equipped at actively ignoring what they believe they need. Eventually, this brings them to a point of mental, emotional, and physical exhaustion. It's normally the moment when they reach out to me.

In our sessions adoptees often tell me, "I don't know who I am," or, "I feel like half of a person and I don't know why." Add to those comments: "I don't want to hurt my adoptive parents, but the truth is that I feel different in a way that is deeply troubling and painful. I feel like an alien in my life."

These descriptions of feeling like an alien, foreigner, or impostor — the raw expression of being different — are all too common in the adoptee community. Even the most open adoptions may find the adoptee searching for a belonging that seems just beyond their reach.

Which brings me to a discussion of the difference between open and closed adoptions and between domestic and international ones. Open adoption is when a child's bio parents and adoptive family have access to varying degrees of each other's personal information and have the option to continue contact on some level. Closed adoption is when bio parents have no direct contact with the adoptee and their adoptive family, and adoptive parents often know little or nothing about their child's first family. In closed adoption, records are sealed — which includes medical information — and information about a child's bio father is most commonly not included, even on the original birth certificate.

Domestic adoption refers to when bio parents, adoptive parents, and the child live in the United States. The process is regulated by state laws and policies. International adoption, also known as intercountry adoption, is when parents adopt a child from a country outside their own and bring that child to live with them. Information about a child's bio family and their medical and social history will vary within international/intercountry adoption depending on the country and culture from which the child originates.

Finally, transracial/transcultural adoption refers to when a child of one race or ethnic group is adopted by parents of another race or ethnic group. In each of these scenarios, it's vitally important that adoptees experience a safe and healthy level of openness as they grow and begin to explore their own internal thoughts, emotions, and questions. In this way, every adoption — no matter the arrangement — has the potential to be more open and every adoptee has the ability to feel less like an alien, foreigner, or impostor in their own life.

I have used all these words at one time or another to describe the intense feelings of marginalization I was living with as an adoptee of a closed and international adoption. These feelings of living on the fringes of my life followed me into adulthood. I felt incurably like an outsider. I didn't know that I had the power to mend the brokenness and reconnect to Julié Dawn. No one ever suggested that I could offer myself that kind of healing salve.

For a very long time I avoided the mere thought of my first me. I told myself that she didn't exist anymore, when deep down inside I knew that was a lie. My first me was an ever-present part of my internal world. Until I was able to make the courageous decision to reconnect to her — to bring her from out of the shadows — I'd continue living as only half of myself.

Take a moment to consider these questions:

1. How can adoptees become whole when they are living only half their story?
2. How can adoptees come home to what is true for them when a bond of communication to their earliest self has not been formed?

Reclamation, Reconnection, and Reintroduction

In my experience the pain of living only half of who I was — the dis-ease of this kind of suffering — became too much, and I had to begin the process of reclamation. *Reclamation*, the process of re-asserting my right to access my truth, and *reconnection*, plugging back in to my earliest self, would require me to reintroduce myself to the purest place of love within me. All paths led to reclaiming my connection to a little girl named Julié Dawn, the child within me I'd long been avoiding. I cannot stress enough my wholehearted belief that, as adoptees, it's vital that we give ourselves the blessing of acknowledging and holding the *both/and* of our experience instead of living an existence of *either/or*.

—⟋⟋—

ADOPTEE AWAKENING: *Love liberates. In order to live free and whole, adoptees must be willing to reconnect to the purest place of love within themselves.*

REFLECTION EXERCISE
Getting Clear in Order to Connect to What Is Real

As you read these words, I ask you to contemplate if you, too, might be avoiding a very real and present part of yourself as an adoptee. Have you been avoiding the child within you who longs to be free? Are you avoiding the earliest parts of yourself, the parts that want to join you in this healing journey? There is absolutely no judgment here. You're safe to speak your truth. I understand. I, too, have traveled this journey of reclamation and reconnection.

Take a moment and reflect on what things you might be holding onto that were once stated or implied about who you are or about the child who awaits within you. How might these outside implications have become the totality of your identity, even if they don't feel true to you? How does that make you feel? How might these implications have caused you to abandon parts of yourself? What do you need to get clear about in order to reclaim those parts? I want to assure you that what feels lost can be found. Don't you think it's time to reconnect to what is true for you?

—◊◊—

ADOPTEE AWAKENING: *Adoptees can reclaim their fullest story. They can take back the self-ownership that they feel was once taken from them.*

Do you want to find the little one — your first me — again? Because that person still lives inside you. And that child needs to be acknowledged, seen, and heard. I've found that the work of healing is best done when the *first me* and the *current me* are united. Are you ready to reclaim your fullest story and identity? Are you willing to own all that you are and all that you're here to be? I'd like to guide you now through an exercise of reclamation and reconnection that I call the Letter of Compassionate Acknowledgment.

REFRAMING EXERCISE
Letter of Compassionate Acknowledgment

This exercise is designed to be the starting point to reconnecting with your earliest self once you've moved through the Welcome to the World Invitation. The Letter of Compassionate Acknowledgment is a letter-writing exercise to the little person inside the adoptee who has experienced so much loss, the little one who has all too often been silenced and hidden somewhere deep inside.

Often adoptees will identify with this child as being the unborn child inside them. They go way back to the womb and access the energy of their experience there. Other times they may see a child of seven or ten years coming forth and wanting to connect. Please know that there is no right or wrong place to start connecting with your first me.

In this exercise we go to the earliest version of ourselves that wants to emerge, and we speak to that child through a letter of acknowledgment and compassion. If you're ready, I'd be honored to guide you through your own process of reconnecting to your earliest me.

As we begin, do a scan of your body and check in. Do you feel safe in your body right now? If you feel at all anxious or nervous, do whatever helps you to safely soothe and find comfort within. I take a walk or spend time with my horses. I'll get out of my head and into my heart in order to self-soothe and self-comfort. Once you feel safe in your body, safe within your surroundings, and ready to write, consider asking yourself these questions:

- What false stories are still living within you, about your earliest self, that are holding you up and making you feel let down or disappointed?

- What stories about your life pre- or postadoption are preventing you from believing that there is more for you in your life?
- What is the real truth that you're here to share — a truth that can only come through reclaiming and reconnecting to your earliest self?
- What's been unfairly pinned to your being that you're ready to shed?

Remember, in this Letter of Compassionate Acknowledgment the focus is on reclaiming your earliest self and earliest truth. Be dedicated to nurturing your well-being as an adoptee. You are here to live as a whole being.

The Process: Letter of Compassionate Acknowledgment

Find a quiet space to sit and be with yourself and your thoughts. Bring a pen and paper with you. Feel free to light candles, if you wish, or to play healing music in the background — whatever you need to ground yourself and settle into this moment.

I will often listen to EMDR music as I write. EMDR music, also known as bilateral music, is music or a series of sounds that travels from left to right — to one ear and then the other. Our attention is called to follow this direction of sound as our brain is stimulated on both sides and communication between the two hemispheres of the brain is strengthened. This type of stimulation aids me in experiencing more free-flowing thoughts, decreases any nervousness I may be experiencing, and increases my relaxation as I write. I make note of EMDR music here as a friendly suggestion that may help support you as you write your Letter of Compassionate Acknowledgment.

Set the Intention and Connect with the Vision

Set the intention for this quiet time of acknowledgment and compassion by saying these words: *I am here to create a clear, comfortable, and safe space to reconnect with my earliest self, to acknowledge this part of me, and to compassionately go inward to this sacred place. I am willing to speak to and hear from the child who still lives within me and who needs to heal along with me.*

Connect with the vision. Close your eyes. Let your vision go to the child who is waiting to come forth. Where is this child? What does this child look like? How old is this child in your vision? Your vision may be vivid, or it may be more abstract, like a feeling you experience or a color you see in your mind's eye. Let your vision be what it wants to be in this moment. Release any judgment that may sneak in by saying: *I choose acceptance over resistance and judgment. I am here to accept and receive, with love and openness, the child who lives within me.*

Begin writing anything and everything that comes to you. Feel what you need to feel as you begin reconnecting to the child within and opening up the lines of communication. You are both safely held in this process.

Let your words flow. There's no need to edit a single sentence! Keep on writing until you've said all you need to say. Let your words be raw and real. There is no length requirement: your letter may be four pages or four sentences long. Just be true to yourself. Honor this time of reconnection.

Once you have completed this exercise, you can hold your letter in your hands and quietly contemplate what has come forth. You can read your letter out loud to yourself, share it with a friend or family member you trust, or reach out to me via my website (TheMichelleMadrid.com), as I'm always here to listen, support, and hear you.

The Healing Power of Yes

In writing your letter, you have begun to say yes to living the fullest expression of who you are. You are saying yes to more meaningful connection with yourself and to deepening your internal dialogue. Embrace the healing power of this yes! Adoptees don't have to live cut off from themselves. They can reclaim and reconnect to their earliest self and create a dynamic, healing friendship with their first me. Adoptees have had to say no to themselves for too long. I want you to feel the beauty of saying yes to yourself, yes to your dreams, and yes to your life. Say yes! Feel the openness of the word.

I have a coaching client who wrote a very simple Letter of Compassionate Acknowledgment to her first me in which she said, "I want to find the little me. I'm still me. Little me and current me will find each other. We will!"

With that simple yet powerful declaration of *yes*, it seemed the universe opened up doors that were once closed. My client received an email containing an unexpected photo of her first me – the baby she was before being adopted. Her plan was to put that photo in a frame and continue connecting and speaking with her first me.

Since reconnecting and reclaiming the child within, my client expresses feeling more grounded, openhearted, accepting, and willing to try new experiences. She no longer lives a closed-off existence. She is learning to merge her biology and biography – to equate the value and the lessons of both – and to understand what that means for her. The result is a woman who feels more complete within herself and is increasingly willing to live on her own terms.

—༄—

ADOPTEE AWAKENING: *Adoptees don't have to live a compartmentalized existence. They are worthy of living fully connected to who they are as they embrace and reconcile with the earliest parts of themselves.*

In the next chapter we'll explore pain point number 2, broken bonds and a deep sense of loss. I'll familiarize you with the five stages of grief. We'll explore how adoptees learn, very early on, to bury their grief. This doesn't have to be the adoptee reality! We'll switch the mute button from on to off, giving ourselves permission to let out the grief — let it go — and free our voices into the light of authentic expression and self-permission.

Adoptee Affirmation

I am capable of reclaiming all that is mine to claim.

Chapter Three

Permission to Grieve

Broken Bonds and a Deep Sense of Loss

I want to begin this chapter by honoring you for moving through the previous exercises of invitation, reclamation, and reconnection. Understanding that we are welcome in our own lives and that we have the power to reclaim what is ours sets a solid foundation for doing the excavation work that lies ahead of us on this soulful healing journey. Remember, as the Maori healer once told me, "Pain is housed in the bones. If we don't do the work of going deep to find it, it causes a state of dis-ease within us."

We need to dig deep in order to reveal all that there is to heal. Adoptees are worthy of doing this excavation work, of looking at their pain, at the wound calling out to be healed. Adoptees are courageous enough to carry out this meaningful task of mending what is broken. They are deserving of a life complete with restoration and renewal. Or, as I like to say, the restoring of ourselves back into ourselves.

As an adult adoptee, the best gift I've given to myself is the permission to dig deep and ask myself why I am the way I am and why I do the things I do. Being curious, without judgment, has offered me so many moments of self-revelation. I know that it takes a ton of work and a huge amount of intentionality, but digging deep and getting to know yourself on a more meaningful level will support you in leading a life that is greater than you ever imagined.

A Few Words on Healing

Stepping onto the pathway of healing means that you're committed to going back, accessing difficult memories and moments, and dedicating yourself to healing those core wounds — some of which have been passed down through the generations. *Healing is ancestral work!* I once read that what you heal for yourself, you heal for your entire family line. I believe this is true.

Healing requires feeling. Pain can't be intellectualized away. When a hurt has been internalized or repressed, we're called to do the brave work of excavating and expressing the pain — mourning out loud — in order to heal those fragmented pieces of ourselves. When we do this, the hurt is put on notice that it will no longer hinder our happiness or control our life. This is the moment when we begin to emerge anew. We launch ourselves into a new frontier of speaking truth, sharing our real and imperfect story, and standing as proof that there is life beyond the pain.

I want to clarify that being healed doesn't mean that the hurt never happened. It means that it did happen but that you didn't run from it. You wrestled with the hurt and walked through it. You pioneered your way through it! Adoptees are heroes of the heart. Commit to being that kind of hero!

As you begin to excavate and express feelings that have been internalized and repressed, it is helpful to distinguish between (1) the feeling and (2) your identity. We can often confuse the two. Here's a quick exercise to help you as you begin awakening to your innermost thoughts and feelings.

EMOTIONAL EXPRESSION EXERCISE

- **Check in.** Ask yourself how you're feeling right now. Doing so will center you in the present moment.
- **Use "I statements" with care.** As you answer your check-in question, practice saying phrases like "I feel confused" rather than saying, "I am confused." You see, you are not confusion. That's not your identity. You are a real person with real feelings, and the feeling you are experiencing in the moment is one of confusion.
- **Focus on the positive.** Once you've identified the feeling you're experiencing, you can ask yourself positive-focused questions like: *What is this feeling here to teach me? How is this feeling here to grow me? What is this feeling here to show me?* Explore and journal on these questions of growth and possibility.
- **Let go of judgment.** Please don't judge yourself or your feelings. With this emotional expression exercise, you are giving yourself permission to be truly seen by first seeing yourself, witnessing your feelings, staying curious about those feelings, and loving yourself through the process.
- **Repeat often.** Make this practice of emotional expression a healing habit.

—꩜—

ADOPTEE AWAKENING: *Healing is ancestral work. What you heal for yourself, you heal for your entire family line, past, present, and future. The process of healing your life, as an adoptee, is just that powerful.*

Speaking the Unspoken

Part of this heroic excavation work is committing ourselves to speaking what is all too often unspoken about adoption and the adoptee experience. I would be remiss if I began this chapter on grief without stating this adoption truth up front: loss is a part of every adoptee story. Loss is at the core of adoption — one family must come apart before another family can come together. A loss had to occur before adoption could ever happen.

For decades and decades, the loss experienced by adoptees has been glossed over because it has been less socially recognized and acceptable. The adoptee's real and human perspective has been widely left out of the conversation. This dynamic is beginning to shift, in many cases, due to the power of social media and its ability to connect the adoptee community on a global level. Adult adoptees worldwide are doing the brave work of sharing what it has been like to be silenced — the pain and isolation of that lived experience. They are speaking out in order to support and hear each other and to help a younger adoptee generation, along with adoptive families, recognize the importance of bringing into the light the points of pain in adoption that historically have been carried in the dark. There is power in the ability to see yourself in another person's story and to feel understood. Adoptees are harnessing the energy of this power, and the dialogue is beginning to be less and less secretive. Even teenage adoptees are speaking more openly with their peers and in their online communities about their deepest thoughts and feelings as they grow up adopted.

Yet for generations, few people outside the adoptee community have wanted to acknowledge, let alone talk about, the *t*-word: *trauma*, which can be defined as any stressful event that is prolonged, overwhelming, or unpredictable. In more spiritual terms, trauma is the unalignment of the true and genuine authentic self because it's been too painful to be that person. Healing, as adoptees, comes through the reconnection to and reclaiming of the genuine and authentic self. This is the work you're doing as you move through the pages of this book.

The very process of family formation, through adoption, that is supposed to be centered on the well-being of a child in need has failed to focus on the traumatic loss the adopted child has experienced. There is trauma in adoption, and there is no shame in saying so! It's imperative that we speak to this truth: the experience of being adopted is not as simple as it's been made out to be.

Adoption is a story of broken primal bonds. A child is removed from her first family and placed in the arms of people she's never met. The child is left with questions, fears, doubts, and anxiety and has no way of openly expressing, verbalizing, or even contextualizing those very real and raw emotions unless sacred space is created for this type of healing release as the child grows.

We must recognize the trauma associated with adoption loss so that we can better support adoptees in answering their questions and healing their unresolved fears, doubts, hurts, and anxiety. As one of my coaching clients, Emily, once shared, "I lost my first self when I was adopted. No one wants to speak to that, and so I was left to wonder — alone — how I could grieve that girl when I still don't even know who I am."

Real, meaningful, transparent conversation about the loss adoptees experience — loss of first self, first family, first identity, first nationality, first language, first culture — has gone against the grain of a simplistic and fairy-tale narrative that has not served to support adoptees, much less prepare adoptive parents for the pain that their child will likely carry.

How tragic it is to hear an adult adoptee share, in a coaching session, "My parents want to control me. While I'm with them, I know that I can't really be me. I am not safe to openly grieve or express my feelings." Or "I know that I can't ever be me until my parents are no longer here on this earth. I'll never be able to process my loss until they're gone." I have had those very same thoughts.

For many years I kept my grief about my adoption hidden. People all around me would say how lucky I was that someone took me in. Their words diminished my sense of worth. I felt like a charity case and not a valued part of the family. On top of that, I didn't feel lucky. I appreciated and loved my adoptive family, yet I silently mourned the first family I had lost. You see, I loved them, too.

Would it be acceptable to say to a nonadopted child who has lost his parents that he is lucky and should be grateful? Would it be okay to pat that child on the shoulder and ask him to just move on? Would it be acceptable to tell that child that the loss of his parents was likely for the best? These are not extreme comparisons to make. You see, these are comments that adoptees hear all the time. It's vital we consider that for adoptees the loss of first parents is akin to a loss experienced through death — yet the loss through adoption is widely seen as not worthy of grieving. This divide leaves adoptees feeling erased and silenced.

Disenfranchised Grief:
Ignore the Loss and Just Be Grateful

There is a kind of grief known as *disenfranchised grief,* and it very much applies to the way that many adoptees experience their loss. Grief becomes disenfranchised when others do not validate or recognize a loss or the subsequent grieving process. Adoptees are told — even today — that they shouldn't be grieving. They should "just be grateful." They shouldn't spend their time wondering about what or who came first. This has been the primary attitude for decades. It's beginning to change as awareness increases, but it's safe to say that the current and widely shared opinion is that adoption is solely a blessing and that adoptees should "just be happy" about it. The result of this one-sided narrative is that adoptees feel like they can't talk about their loss and their grief. They can't find support. They feel completely alone as they're told what they should or shouldn't feel.

When I was a young adoptee, my mother would often tell me to "just be grateful" whenever I tried to express the grief that kept swirling around inside me. She'd say, "I saved you from a really hard place, so you should move on and just be grateful." In our inner dialogue, adoptees ask ourselves: *Where do you go to grieve when you're continually told that you must be grateful for being saved? Where do you turn when your adoption story feels more centered on the emotions and beliefs of the parents who adopted you? How will anyone ever really know you? How will you ever really know yourself?* Adoptees learn very early on to bury their grief, to turn it off and disconnect. They have, sometimes all their lives, been deprived of the grieving process — a process that is fundamental to healing. Their grief is disenfranchised. This lack of support can prolong the adoptee's emotional pain.

Here's something I know for sure: buried and disenfranchised grief only serves to bury the adoptee's spirit — their light — deep within the broken bonds of their story. We can't openly experience what we need to feel in order to move forward in our lives. Our loss, along with our need to grieve and mourn that loss, takes a back seat.

Disenfranchised grief can turn into depression, anxiety, and PTSD, among other ailments. This sense of dis-ease grows as the adoptee continues the internal housing of their hurt. It feels like there is no way out. Perhaps this is why adoptees often feel so misunderstood. They've been forced into living a narrative that feels, at best, partially false and, at worst, completely false. You see, adoptees aren't ungrateful for their lives — they just need to safely and openly grieve their loss.

Here's a question for consideration: Even if an adoptee is content, can they still be allowed space to honor their first me, to honor where they came from, and to embrace who they were before they were adopted? Can adoptees, no matter their perspective and experience, be given the space to explore both the shadow and the shine of their adoptee journey? As a society we have lost and stand to lose much more if we don't give adoptees the opportunity to explore all sides of their story — the biology and biography of who they are — and to grieve, express, and process their loss.

Sit with this sobering statistic: adoptees living in the United States are nearly four times more likely to lose their life to suicide than nonadoptees. This particular statistic comes from a study done at the University of Minnesota. The participants involved were drawn from the Sibling Interaction and Behavior Study, conducted between 1998 and 2008. Increasingly, studies in other countries are identifying the need for more research into suicide rates and adoption. In 2022 Australia released an important report: *Intercountry Adoption and Suicide in Australia*. The meta-analysis conducted found that intercountry adoptees in Australia carried twice the risk for suicide attempt, compared to nonadoptees. This report holds great relevance both within Australia's borders and beyond. For example, it notes that studies carried out in Nordic countries have mirrored the results found in the Minnesota study. Further takeaways of the report from Australia include the barriers that intercountry adoptees face over communicating openly about their adoption experience, the disconnect between how an adoptee is expected to feel about being adopted and how they actually feel, and the impact of racism, discrimination, and microaggressions toward intercountry adoptees. Ultimately, the report recommends that guidelines that include the experiences of adoptees be developed to help inform interventions for adoptees who are at risk and to increase overall awareness.

How many bright and promising adoptee souls have left us far too early because their loss and their grief were never considered, acknowledged, or safely held? How many have never received the compassionate and care-filled healing that they so richly deserve?

Every October 30, Adoptee Remembrance Day, the adoptee community pauses and remembers those we have lost. We remember, and we renew our commitment to make more transparent the multilayered experience of being adopted. We hope that, in so doing, we can help those who are struggling to feel less alone. As people who love adoptees, we can begin to help empower them — and yes, even save their lives — by saying to them: *I know that your loss is real. I know that your grief is real. How can I support you? How can I help you?* Check in on an adoptee you love today.

It's also vitally important that we encourage adoptees to say these words to themselves. As adoptees, we must be willing to participate in our own rescue, to acknowledge our loss, allow ourselves to grieve out loud, and ask for support and help. Community is key along the journey of healing. I've learned, firsthand, that it's difficult, if not impossible, to heal alone.

—◊◊◊—

ADOPTEE AWAKENING: *Disenfranchised grief is real. Adoptees don't have to ignore their loss and just be grateful. They can reach out for help. Acknowledge the loss. Process the grief. Feel what is real. This is how adoptees begin to heal.*

When adoptees cannot openly speak to their loss, the negative consequences can impact every aspect of life and chip away at any sense of self-worth. Adoptees describe feeling disposable, invisible, confused about their heritage or identity, afraid to connect, disempowered, depressed, unwanted, unwelcome, angry, distrusting, insecure, ashamed, scared, trapped, and sad.

The fallout from these emotions shows up in a variety of ways over the course of a lifetime. In our coaching sessions, adoptees have expressed this fallout in these terms: living life at arm's distance, being prone to bolt when they feel rejection looming, not knowing how to ask for what they need, judging themselves harshly, worrying about being seen as inadequate in some way, speaking or thinking negatively, isolating themselves, being fiercely independent and unwilling to ask for help, avoiding self-care, and feeling incapable of intimacy. The unresolved trauma of adoption loss will keep showing up, over and over again, unless adoptees are given space to acknowledge and speak to the loss that feels very much in control of their life.

Alexandra Was Wrecked by Disney

My coaching client Alexandra described feeling the fallout of unresolved loss while watching Disney movies as a child. "When I was a kid, I cried at Disney movies every single time. I couldn't bear to see those films when it seemed that the mother always died, or the baby animal was so often separated from its parents. I would come unglued. My adoptive mother would tell me that I was too sensitive. I felt so ashamed of my tears. Mom didn't understand why these movies caused me to panic inside. She just kept bringing me back to more movies, thinking that at some point I'd be stronger and able to sit through them. Those movies wrecked me emotionally! After we'd get home from the theater, I would stay in my bed for hours and hours, weeping. Now when I look back, I think I was mourning my earliest loss and I just didn't know. Mom didn't know, either."

Alexandra early on was experiencing the pain of broken bonds and a deep sense of loss:

- She was panicked when watching an animated Disney character go through the loss of a parent or the experience of being abandoned because it triggered her own sense of loss and abandonment.
- She felt that to be loved and accepted by her adoptive

mother was conditional on her being less sensitive and learning not to cry or become emotional during these movie outings.

• She didn't feel seen, heard, or known in these moments with her mother and was unable to authentically voice her pain or identify and process the grief she felt inside.

When Alexandra first came to me as an adult adoptee, she ranked pain point number 2, the pain of broken bonds and a deep sense of loss, at a 10 on the scale. She described herself this way: "I'm afraid to share my deepest feelings because what if that makes the people I love leave, too? I feel angry about that! Why can't I have a life that is happy, connected, and joy filled? Why can't I be a person who feels excited about my life, my relationships, my work and purpose? I don't even know what my purpose is. I don't even know what I'm here for. Maybe I'm just as lost as those characters in the Disney films. Will I ever find my way home? Sometimes I think I'm just a mistake. Does God make mistakes?"

I could feel Alexandra's anger and anguish. I reminded her that the ability to express her feelings, in that moment, was a significant step forward. She had acknowledged her emotions, which meant that she had stopped resisting and avoiding them. In the process, she became aware that her emotional response to those Disney films, along with the confusion and anger she felt, was evidence of an innocent adoptee who was in the midst of grieving the broken bonds and loss of her adoption story.

—ᴍ—

ADOPTEE AWAKENING: *Adoptees aren't "angry adoptees." It's not their identity. They are adoptees who are grieving and experiencing and expressing anger, a real human emotion and one of the five stages of grief.*

The Five Stages of Grief

Based on psychiatrist Elisabeth Kübler-Ross's model, five stages of grief are most commonly observed, and reviewing them here will give us a much better understanding of the adoptee grieving process. These five stages represent the emotions experienced when faced with loss or impending loss. It should be noted that these stages are not linear and that a person can experience all, some, or none of them during their grieving process. Understanding that adoption is rooted in loss and that the unborn adoptee experiences a sense of impending loss within the womb, it could be argued that for the adopted person, the grieving process may very well begin before they are even born. I have tailored these five stages of grief to the adoptee experience and the unique and nuanced ways adoptees may process their grief.

Denial. It's not unusual for an adoptee to respond to their strong feelings of grief by pretending that the loss never happened. Denial can look like avoidance, confusion, elation, shock, and fear. When I was a young girl, I used to deny that my first parents had left me. I told my friends that my first parents were the queen of England and the king of Spain. They were just too busy with their duties to have me with them. This was my fantasy story — a way of pacing my feelings of grief by living in a preferred reality over an actual one.

Denial is a coping mechanism that can assist the adopted person in numbing the intensity of their grief. Although denial does help us cope with and survive a grief event like adoption loss, prolonged avoidance of emotions can hinder the healing process. This is why it's critical that adoptees are supported in understanding their grief and reminded of the importance of not running from it. Once denial starts to fade, the healing process can begin.

As you move out of the denial stage, the emotions you may have been avoiding or suppressing start coming to the surface. Anger might start to set in.

Anger. Once an adoptee starts to live in an actual and not a preferred reality, anger may start to surface. Anger can look like frustration, irritation, and anxiety. This is the stage of grief where an adoptee may think, "Why me?" and "Life's not fair!" Adoptees may find it incomprehensible that this loss has happened to them. They may question God and wonder why God allowed this loss to occur. Most mental health professionals agree that anger is a necessary stage of grief and that it's important to feel it. In fact, the more you are able to feel the anger, the more quickly it will lessen and the more quickly you will begin to heal. The bottom line is this: it's not healthy for an adoptee to suppress anger. Anger can ground an adoptee and build a bridge back to reality and connection.

My anger, for quite some time, was masked as intense frustration. Much of that frustration was over the fact that I'd been adopted into a family with an alcoholic parent. I felt frustrated that I'd been taken from one challenging situation and placed into another challenging, even volatile, one. This also caused intense anxiety for me. "If social workers were going to remove me, why couldn't they at least have moved me into a home that feels safe?" I felt treated unfairly, and my indignation grew inside me like a cancer. I bottled those feelings up for a long time, which didn't serve me. Once I understood that anger was a necessary response to my early trauma, I clearly saw the importance of finding a safe space to let it out.

I want to clarify that not every adoptee will experience the anger stage of grief. Others may be in this stage for a short time, while some adoptees may linger in it. It's also important to clarify that this stage of grief can be experienced to different degrees and intensities.

Bargaining. Have you ever caught yourself trying to make a deal with God when something bad or unfortunate happens? For the adoptee, this may look like, "Please, God, if you bring back my first parents, I promise to always be a good girl and I'll go to church and never complain." This is bargaining. It's a type of negotiation in the hope of avoiding grief. It's not uncommon for the adoptee to look for ways to regain a sense of control, through bargaining, when so much of their lived experience feels out of their control. It's the "if you change this, I'll change that" approach, along with statements of "what if" and "if only." Adoptees may feel so desperate to go back to life before their adoption that they are willing to make major life changes. Bargaining may look like guilt or struggling to find meaning.

During this stage in my own grieving journey, I made many attempts at negotiation with God. "Please stop my father from drinking, and I promise to be the best daughter and never feel sad about being adopted again." I also made countless "what if" and "if only" statements to myself. When I'd visit my first mother in England, I'd often find myself in her garden, asking myself, *What if I'd been able to stay with Mum?* I'd close my eyes and see a different version of me playing there in the garden. I'd see that girl smelling the flowers and soaking up an English summer sun. The temporary joy I felt while diving into that imaginary space postponed the feelings of sadness and hurt that were stored up inside.

Before we move on to the next stage of grief, I want to note that anger and bargaining can feel very active, as if you're always running and trying to stay a step ahead of the grief as you work to grasp hold of meaning. But the fourth stage of grief, depression, can feel very quiet. Sometimes adoptees isolate themselves in order to cope.

Depression. Depression is perhaps the most well-known form of grief. It can look like overwhelm, flight, helplessness, and hostility. Depression can be very difficult and messy. In this stage, adoptees may withdraw from life, feel numb, and experience fogginess, heaviness, or confusion. Their adoptee journey may feel too overwhelming to face. As much as depression is associated with grief, for adoptees it is often overlooked since the wider narrative suggests that adoptees have nothing to grieve, so why would they be depressed?

In the depression stage, adoptees may not feel like talking, they may not want to be in social settings, and they may feel a deep sense of hopelessness. They may even wonder if there is any point to going on. I want to stress here that if you're an adoptee and can't seem to navigate your way out of this fourth stage of grief, it's vital to reach out to someone you trust who can help you work through this period of depression. Reach out today! You are not alone.

Acceptance. With acceptance, the last stage of grief, adoptees aren't feeling "it's okay that I'm adopted" but rather "I'm adopted, and I'm going to be okay." Acceptance can look like exploring options, putting a new plan in place, or moving on in life. With acceptance, the adoptee's emotions may begin to stabilize as they come to terms with their adoption story. Acceptance represents a time of adjustment and readjustment as the adoptee recognizes that there will be a flow of good days and bad days but that the good days will tend to outnumber the bad ones. Adoptees may begin to reengage with life as they move forward and evolve into a new reality.

In this stage you may hear adoptees saying that they're "coming out of the fog." This expression reflects the period when adoptees begin to emerge from a sense of disconnection and confusion and to awaken to their own thoughts and feelings about being adopted. They then begin to take ownership of those things. For me, FOG means "frequently observing grief." It's a time when adoptees begin to witness their grief — the hidden parts of themselves and the hurts that have been buried deep. Consider the power of light — it burns off fog. Light makes things clear. When adoptees bring the grieving parts of themselves into the light, clarity begins to set in. Their points of pain are transformed into points of light, light that directs them forward into a place of thriving, not just surviving. For me this emerging felt as if I were finally awakening into a truth that I'd longed to live out loud. I began to see myself more clearly. I was separating from the heavy mist that had reduced my self-visibility for so long. I was escorting myself through a mental and emotional fog and moving forward. In my personal and professional experience, coming out of the fog is a highly empowering and transformational time for adoptees.

I am so proud of how you are working your way through this book and the very real emotions of the adoptee experience. For you to be willing to recognize and identify where you may be in the grieving process is remarkable. You're taking ownership of your emotions and doing so in a way that feels best for you, as you express your grief and mourn unresolved loss. I see you!

As discussed in chapter 2, start doing whatever helps you feel safe in your body as you experience these parts of your grieving self. Some adoptees will take up crafts from their country of origin; others will make it a daily practice to sip a warm cup of tea and watch the sun come up as they affirm themselves and their ability to heal. Some adoptees may connect more with music, while others may run marathons or take to meditation and long walks in nature. I am all for adoptees doing whatever they need that is healthy and whole to bring themselves more into their body, as they connect ever deeper with their truest feelings and their power to move through grieving and arrive at a place of relief. A place of light! When I explained the five stages of grief to Alexandra, and when she discovered that anger was one of the stages, it all began to make sense to her. She recognized that she was a grieving adoptee and that safely expressing her anger gave her traction along the path to healing.

As you move toward self-truth, self-acceptance, and self-permission as an adoptee, I'd like to introduce you to the two empowering statements that I use and also share with those I coach: the Adoptee Declaration of Acceptance and the Adoptee Statement of Self-Permission. I offer these tools to help you center yourself and align with your power. I also encourage you to create your own declaration of acceptance and statement of self-permission that you can refer to anytime you need. They are beautiful and affirming practices.

Adoptee Declaration of Acceptance

Say these words of acceptance with me:

> *I fully accept myself — who I am and where I am in this moment — even though I'm still grieving. I fully accept myself, even though a part of me feels like it was cheated out of years with my first family, first identity, first culture, first heritage. I accept that I'm moving through the five stages of grief and that I'll come out on the other side stronger and wiser. I acknowledge these emotions as I support myself through feeling them. I vow not to let these emotions become debilitating ever again. I promise to seek and accept support from those I feel safe to share with. I will accept the tools and resources that I need to increase my sense of self-compassion as I grieve and heal.*

Come back to this Adoptee Declaration of Acceptance as often as you need to. Anytime you need to remind yourself that you are capable of absolute self-acceptance and love, come back to these words. When you need a reminder that grieving is a journey, say these words out loud. This declaration, or one you write for yourself, holds the intention to be your anchor.

—⁂—

ADOPTEE AWAKENING: *Avoiding or resisting the grieving process doesn't support adoptees and leads to a heaviness inside*

that can be hard to define. Adoptees cannot truly be free until
this heaviness is lifted. And the lifting of this internal weight
begins with giving yourself permission to grieve.

Giving Voice to the Soul

I believe in the power of self-permission. Or, as I like to call it, giving voice to the soul. It's a life-affirming practice, one where we begin to grow and blossom in miraculous ways as we permit our truth to emerge.

Recently, I was coaching a child adoptee who lives in Europe. We were talking about the garden at her school, where she's growing potatoes, onions, and tomatoes in her individual gardening plot. I asked her what she'd learned from her experience as a gardener. "For example," I said, "gardens need water to thrive." She replied, "They need the sun, too." I answered, "Indeed, gardens need sunshine to grow." There was a slight pause, then this beautiful little girl said, "And mostly gardens need love."

The voice of this child's soul was speaking. Within a safe space of permission to say and feel all that was coming up from within herself, she spoke words of beauty, wisdom beyond her years, and unconditional love.

Just like that little girl's garden at school, every adoptee has an internal garden. We may not grow vegetables there, but we can grow a beautiful inner ecosystem that supports and nurtures us. We can give ourselves permission to nurture our inner garden — the soil of our soul — with unconditional love, kind words and thoughts, the visualization of colors and places that make us feel good, and anything else that supports us. Part of nurturing our internal garden, as adoptees, is allowing for the safe processing of emotions that are asking to be acknowledged so that we may plant the seeds of transformation and growth.

Now I'd like to share the Adoptee Statement of Self-Permission with you. These words can become an essential part of your daily practice as you tend the soil of your soul, pruning any emotions from your inner garden that do not serve your growth, and seeding within yourself all that is nourishing to your soul. Again, I urge you to create your own statement of self-permission. You can use the one below or write your own; either way, words of self-permission are important to speak as you move into the next reframing exercise, the Story of Your Grief.

Adoptee Statement of Self-Permission

I am safe to feel all that's coming up for me in this moment. I give myself permission to feel and to grieve. I am safely held as I sit here wrapped in the warmth of my body. I am open to feeling the breadth of who I am. I am willing to honor my real feelings because they are valid and worthy. I make a promise to release any emotions of disservice that have been bottled up inside me. I am ready to safely let them flow. Within the flowing, there is cleansing. Within the flowing, there is clarity. I am ready for clarity. I understand that I grieve because I love. In the grieving process, I am loving myself. I am honoring myself. I am remembering who I am. I am listening to my soul. I am finding my way home. And I give myself permission to feel it all.

—⚬⚬⚬—

ADOPTEE AWAKENING: *Healing starts with permission to grieve what's been lost.*

REFRAMING EXERCISE
The Story of Your Grief

The Story of Your Grief exercise guides you in communicating directly with your grief, supporting you through the grieving process as you begin to soften any defense mechanisms so that you may safely excavate whatever's beneath them.

This exercise will ask you to speak to those places inside you where you may be experiencing denial, anger, bargaining, depression, and/or acceptance – in other words, the five stages of grief that we must acknowledge in order to move forward. As challenging as it may at first seem, adoptees must feel all these things in order to process their loss and arrive at a place of peace with all that has been removed from their lives along their adoption journey. When adoptees begin softening those defense mechanisms and safely excavating what is beneath them, they offer themselves the space to truly heal.

A few months ago I received a message from an adult adoptee who wrote, "A P-51 warplane gets a wingman to support him. Adoptees frequently and qualitatively lack this kind of support." What a spot-on piece of perspective! For decades, adoptees have lacked a safe space to navigate their emotional battles as they move through their grief. The feeling that someone has their back has been absent for most. Adoptees are beginning to offer themselves and each other this same sense of support. It's imperative that we become each other's wingmen and that we become our own wingman, too.

Meditation Exercise

Before we begin the Story of Your Grief exercise, I'd like to guide you through a meditation. I offer this meditation so that you can set your focus on being supported and safely cared for. I want you not only to know but to feel that you are not alone. Meditation can help you connect to that feeling and to an increased sense of awareness.

First, sit comfortably in a chair, then close your eyes and

take a deep breath in. Feel your breath – know that you are breathing in.

Now, release your breath with a long, slow exhale. Feel the exhale of your breath – know that you are breathing out.

With your eyes still closed, imagine a plane in the sky. What does the plane look like? See the colors and designs both on the exterior and the interior of the plane. See yourself sitting in the pilot's seat and looking out at the earth below. Perhaps you notice clouds floating beneath you. You may even see the shadow of the aircraft dancing across the landscape as you fly.

At first it appears as if you're the only one in the sky. You wonder, *Is anyone else out there?* Then suddenly another plane appears, seemingly out of nowhere. It carefully moves from behind you and positions itself by your side. You look over and see another pilot, who gives you a kind nod of acceptance and knowing, as if to say, *You are not alone. I offer my support and safe passage home.* You feel a sense of peace and belonging as you fly onward to new possibilities. You may even feel a sense of empowerment as you pilot your plane forward with your wingman by your side.

Stay with this feeling of belonging as long as you like. Allow yourself to experience the sensation of being supported and guided. Let the feeling comfort you – let it be the wind beneath your wings. That's it. Let the feeling move through your body and center you. Let this feeling of belonging connect you to a sense of safety. You are safe here.

When you're ready, and there's no rush, you can open your eyes to the room. Stay connected to the feeling you experienced in the meditation.

As you read the prompts for the Story of Your Grief exercise, I'd like you to think of these prompts as your wingmen. They are offered as a support to safely guide you as you navigate the grieving process and identify which of the five stages of grief you are experiencing.

Be kind to yourself as you move through this reframing exercise. Be gentle with yourself as you explore what's beneath the grief. You've already faced many challenging emotions along this adoption journey. Don't be afraid to face your grief. Honor how it shows up for you, and allow those feelings to move through you.

As you begin this exercise, please keep a glass of water nearby so that you stay hydrated. And, of course, a tissue or two may be needed as you release emotions that may have been bottled up for quite some time. You can go back to the Adoptee Declaration of Acceptance and the Adoptee Statement of Self-Permission if you feel, at any time, a resistance to releasing all that is waiting to be set free.

Let's begin. Start by reflecting on where you may be within the five stages of grief: denial, anger, bargaining, depression, and acceptance. Remember, when you acknowledge your emotions, you become stronger and more empowered. You begin to understand your feelings more clearly as you allow yourself to process all that's been bottled up inside you. Again, no judgment. As adoptees, we are here to better understand ourselves and the grieving process. We are here to love ourselves in this way as we begin to truly see ourselves.

Feel free to explore this exercise in any way you'd like. You may want to tell the Story of Your Grief through dance or another kind of movement that feels good to you. Perhaps you'd like to experience your story of grief through creating an original piece of music or singing an original song. You may want to play an instrument, paint, sculpt, or write poetry. You may prefer to continue writing in a journal as your means of expression, or creating sacred space for a ritual of your choice. You may even want to partake in a meaningful cultural or religious practice. As mentioned earlier, some of my internationally adopted coaching clients connect with their grief while doing a craft from their country of origin. You may want to create a collage of images that help tell your story. You might pour yourself a cup of warm tea and soak in a hot bath as you speak your story out loud. You may choose to take a long hike or run, exploring nature as you experience your story coming forward.

This is your story to tell. The focus should be on allowing your feelings to arise as you give voice to your grief and safely feel your emotions. The goal is to dialogue with the grieving parts of yourself in order to understand them more deeply as you witness the wisdom that awaits you in this place.

The following twelve questions are prompts to help you gently begin connecting to the Story of Your Grief. Let these questions be your wingmen, guiding you along in this journey of communication with your grief. Allow them to help transform your grief into a power you never knew you possessed.

Prompts for the Story of Your Grief

1. What stage of grief am I currently in?
2. What has been my primary story about this stage of grief?
3. How is my grief showing up in my life and in my relationships?
4. What wisdom waits for me within my grieving parts? What is this wisdom here to teach me? How is it here to grow me? What is it here to show me?
5. What parts of my grieving story have caused me to feel unsafe or uncertain?
6. How has my story caused me to view love as conditional?
7. How have I had to mask my authentic feelings of

grief? How has this masking separated me from a deeper knowing of who I am?

8. Who do I want to be beyond the grief? What's my vision?

9. How can moving through my grief reconnect me to the life I deserve and to a sense of safety, calm, and unconditional love?

10. How can I use this wisdom to reignite my life?

11. How can I write a brand-new story, one that ignites a whole new way of being?

12. What does that new story look like for me?

I hope these prompts support you as you continue to explore the story of your grief. Take time with this exercise. Allow yourself to journey through these questions and to listen for what the wisdom of your grief wants to say. Here's one thing I know for sure: there is insight to be found here. Our wounds hold a world of wisdom! When we avoid our grieving, we delay our growing. Indeed, when you tell the story of your grief, you begin to write the story of your growth.

I want to assure you that grieving loss is a part of the adoptee journey. I also want to assure you that mourning your loss is vital. It's sacred. You can approach this process in your own time and in the way that feels most supportive to you. My hope is that society will begin to hold more space for this truth: adoptees grieve their loss and they need to mourn their loss. They grieve because they love. Your grief is your unexpressed love. The process of acknowledging adoptee grief can be a life-affirming outreach of self-love. It can also be a profound recognizing and acknowledging of what came before the adoptee's adoption.

Expressing the grief that has gone unsaid offers a roadmap toward healing and sewing up our wounds. Dearest adoptee, be a warrior for your grief because that is how we, as a community of real, breathing people, move from a place of suffering to a beautiful state of living and thriving.

You are not alone in the grieving process. I can't say that enough! You can safely explore your emotions. You can feel your feelings. You can speak to your hurt and listen for the wisdom that comes from the wound. You can walk through your grief and on to a place of full, unapologetic self-acceptance. We can do this together!

As I moved my client Alexandra through the five stages of grief, and as she reflected on the grieving process through the Story of Your Grief exercise, she accepted herself and where she was in the process. As a result, her pain point moved from a 10 to a 3 just with those simple yet effective tools. These tools assisted Alexandra in softening her protection mechanisms — opening herself to vulnerability and honesty — in order to get to what was waiting beneath. It's in honoring our journey, as adoptees, and in voicing our deepest feelings that we heal the grief we've harbored within us often since childhood.

I want you to know that you are not, and never have been, a mistake. Your life is on purpose and for purpose. You are innocent of the circumstances surrounding your story. Those circumstances do not define you. Please, keep this truth close to your heart. It will support you in navigating this adoptee journey.

I'm rooting for you and encouraging you to keep moving forward. I want you to feel my love and to know that I care as you move through your grief and onward to growth. I also want you to know just how proud I am of you. I will always be your wing(wo)man!

Love and connection are basic human needs. Sometimes we resist because we feel too vulnerable letting ourselves believe that someone truly cares about us. As an adoptee, I understand that kind of resistance. Yet it is essential that we view ourselves as worthy of love and connection — first by seeing and loving ourselves. Honoring our grief is how we begin to see and love ourselves as adopted people. It's a pure gift to allow yourself to be seen in all your beautiful vulnerability. When you allow your truth to be seen, you even inspire others to identify and see their own.

As you continue to gently move through your grief, with kindness and compassion for yourself, don't hesitate to reach out to others if you need additional support. Reach out to me, seek therapeutic adoption-focused counseling, or ask for understanding from a trusted loved one. Read books on the topic of grief and grieving, and connect with other adoptees along this journey. The adoptee experience involves complex emotions. Nothing is more powerful than hearing the words *I understand. I get it. I've been there, too.* Connecting on this level of understanding — adoptee to adoptee — is very special. Lean in! Please know that you can return to the Story of Your Grief exercise whenever you need to connect with just how far you've come. It's a place you can land to remind yourself of all that awaits you as you grow through your grief.

In the next chapter we'll explore pain point number 3, not knowing: the pain of being denied access to truth. We'll access your power key to unlocking your truth. I believe that everything adoptees need to heal their pain and access their truth can be found within them right now. Adoptees have the power to heal; they've just become detached from this place of power. When so much of an adopted person's sense of self is stripped away through abandonment and removal, and when so much of their life narrative is assigned to them by outside sources, it can feel as if the key to their power has been knocked out of their hands. Through a priming exercise, I'll guide you to bring that key back into your possession and arrive at a place of deep and meaningful knowing.

Adoptee Affirmation

I grieve because I love. My love is immense.
My grief is a reflection of love's immensity.

Chapter Four

Not Knowing

The Pain of Being Denied Access to Truth

"The truth will set you free." I recited these words at least a thousand times while growing up in the Methodist Church and reading scripture from the book of John. I believed in these words. When I was thirteen and preparing for my confirmation — the public sealing of the covenant created in baptism — I asked the pastor of my church if there was a sin that could not be forgiven. He replied, "The only sin that cannot be forgiven is to deny the truth. It's like seeing a rose in front of you and denying that the rose exists."

Beyond being an object of faith, truth is also defined as the actuality of things or events, and as facts or reality. Other definitions concern sincerity, a quality that bears the fruit of trust. The opposite of truth, then, would be lies, falsity, fiction, and falsehood. Human beings, adopted or not, hold an intrinsic desire for truth. Without truth, it is difficult to answer the questions, *Who am I? Why am I here?* and *What is my purpose?* In other words, without truth it's extremely challenging to feel free to become who we're here to be.

That moment with my pastor was pivotal. I was a young adoptee who felt that the denial of truth — facts and reality — was deeply woven into the fabric of my adoption story. I knew that the truth of my existence was still a secret to many. I knew somehow that I was not being offered the complete truth from those around me. I also felt unsafe to openly speak the truth of my real feelings. Life as an adoptee felt very much like a tale of lies, falsity, fiction, and falsehoods. How could I trust anyone or anything when truth wasn't freely given and received? This is an important question to contemplate as we move forward because, as many adoptees will tell you, a life void of truth makes it nearly impossible to trust and to thrive.

Before we delve deeper into this topic, I want to acknowledge the work you just completed in chapter 3: the acceptance you're speaking, the self-permission you're giving, and the connection you're forging with your grieving parts through creating your own story of grief. You're freeing your voice and exploring the truth that lives within you. Your truth! This is brave work, and I want you to know that I'm holding loving space for you, in these pages, as we move forward together.

Let me emphasize that adoptees are a population of people that has, over countless decades, been denied their basic rights of freedom of information and access to the truth. This is a recurring pain point that creates a serious sense of dis-ease within the adoptee community. Adoptees have been told that they don't need to know the truth of their own human story. They've been instructed not to linger in the past. This is part of a major disconnect within the adoption conversation; what others may deem as being in the past, the adoptee regards as still present and very much alive.

Listen to the words of Sabrina, an adult adoptee recently coming out of the fog — awakening to herself and to her truth as an adopted person — as she explains the lack of adoption information she'd been living with: "I have no record of who I am. People who aren't adopted don't really understand what that's like. The things they take for granted — like a birth certificate — I don't have. It's a huge void."

Here's one thing I know for sure: selective truth is not truth at all. Yet, time and time again many adoptees are offered pieces of truth that don't quite fit together. It's like constructing a puzzle with missing pieces. The adoptee who possesses little to no information about their earliest life may have thoughts like, *Surely, the missing pieces exist! Those pieces are out there somewhere, right? Who holds those missing pieces to my story? Why are the pieces being hidden from me? I feel helpless. There are so many holes, how will I ever be complete?*

For adoptees, not knowing can be the hardest part of their journey. To be denied access to truth feels like a violation. One adoptee shared with me in a coaching consultation: "I just want to know my roots. How dare someone withhold information that is mine to know? Why would they lock me out? I don't want to hurt anyone, but it seems unfair that it's acceptable to hurt me. I live with this overwhelming sense of being wounded, and it impacts everything I do."

That's what denial of information, of the truth, feels like to the adoptee: a wound that can't be healed, a wound that is constantly ripped open as the adoptee is denied access to birth records, medical records, foster records, and more. Even a routine doctor's appointment can hurt. It's that moment when the nurse asks, "And what about your family medical history?" The adoptee may reply, "I don't know my medical history" or, "I have very little information on that. I'm adopted."

The nurse's response goes something like this: "That's okay. I'll just leave that section blank." And then there's the pause. The one that makes an adopted person ache inside as they're reminded of all the information they long to have. It's a pause that feels dehumanizing and deflating. It's an intrusive interruption that tears open the wound — time and time again.

As another adoptee shared with me, "Every single time that I hold a medical form in my hand and have to fill it out, I am forced to openly declare the pain of my loss on a piece of paper. Having to write something like 'Family Health History Unknown — Adopted' feels like a punch straight to the gut and a slap directly in the face. Everything about me feels unknown and lost. I wish people could understand." This adoptee's wish is shared by much of the larger adoptee community — the wish that others might someday understand just how wounded adopted people feel when they're left to wonder, with little hope, if the facts of their earliest story will ever be revealed to them.

You Don't Need to Know

"You don't need to know." These five words have been extremely harmful to so many adoptees over the decades, yet they are still spoken to and around adopted people. These words, or some variation on them, have caused adoptees — for generations — to feel hopelessly trapped in pain point number 3.

When a person is left to plead for their personal information, what they hear instead of "you don't need to know" is "you don't deserve to know." Adoptees have been told for far too long that they don't deserve to know the people, places, and facts of their earliest story. That part of who they are has been locked away by the outside world.

When I embarked on the process of obtaining my foster records from the United Kingdom, it took me a full nine months to prove that I was mentally and emotionally fit to see and read the facts of my own story. I had to convince those who held the power over my records that I deserved and could handle the truth held within those documents. It took me nine long months to unlock the locked pages of Julié Dawn's earliest experience. Nine stressful months of birthing the truths of my time in foster care back into my hands, where they belonged.

Fighting to access foster and adoption records can be a long and arduous process filled with legal firewalls, letter writing, fee paying, petitioning of courts, and demonstrating capacity. It's not fair, in this adoptee's eyes, but it's the reality I'd been living — a reality so many adoptees live with. Freedom of information, in the adoptee's world, is far from free.

After I had finally proven my ability to read my own story, the foster records arrived to me via airmail from the United Kingdom. They came organized in a plain green folder. I don't know what I was expecting — maybe a more formal presentation that represented the work I'd put in to claim my records? Instead, my story was waiting for me inside a simple plastic file.

I was a grown woman holding, for the first time, the truths of my relinquishment and adoption. Truths that could have eased so much anxiety and confusion, had I been given the opportunity of knowing them earlier on. My hands trembled as I read the cover of the file: Birth Name — Julié Dawn. As I opened the folder, I reminded myself to breathe. It was like stepping back in time and into a place that I had longed to revisit. I sat down on my couch and began to comb through the pages in my file detailing the physical and emotional traits of my bio parents, their birth dates and birth places, their occupations and hobbies.

My foster records went on to detail the dynamics of my first parents' relationship at the time, and their reaction to the news of me. My mother had always told me that her affair with my father was "one night only." She depicted that chapter in her life as a lonely one and told me that my father had taken advantage of her loneliness. When I asked my mother for details about my father, she'd simply respond, "I don't remember." This lack of information always left me feeling lesser than. I believed that somehow my father was bad, and I carried that feeling with me for years.

What I learned from my foster records was that my mother and father's relationship had gone on for months. It was not a one-night stand. They were two consenting adults who shared a bond. My father even played with my mother's three children. He would come to her home and throw a ball with her kids, in the garden. I never had that opportunity to laugh and play with my dad. Once I read my foster records, I couldn't help but wonder why my first father would play with my mother's children but would choose to leave me, his own daughter, behind.

Margaret and Juliáno were my parents. They were also a mother and father who decided not to keep me. No one involved had a preference for my religious upbringing. My mother told me that she had specified that I not be adopted outside the United Kingdom, yet I became an international adoptee through my adoption into America.

I remember phoning my mother when I finished reviewing my foster records, so many years after my relinquishment. "Mum," I said, "I have my foster records now and I've read a more complete story of what happened. I wasn't the product of a one-night-only moment, was I? You and my father had a deeper connection. Somehow, that makes a difference to me. I don't know why, but it matters to me that I know."

My mother replied, "Well, I'm happy you know the truth now." That's all she said. I replied, "Yes, Mum, the truth will set you free." I hung up the phone and cried. I cried for the little girl spoken about in my foster file. It was as if the child wasn't human. She was, indeed, looked on as a matter for my country of origin to settle. England did its job. I was adopted and sent on my way.

Reading the facts of my earlier story — even though they were hard to see — was liberating. I needed to know and, yes, I deserved to know! Those once-missing pieces to my story had been found. My life puzzle felt a little more complete. I felt a little less wounded. For the first time I saw my first parents as real people in a messy and difficult situation. They were not perfect. My first parents were not characters from a fairy tale. They weren't royalty. They were both flawed and human, just like me. This truth made me feel a little less like damaged goods and a little more like a daughter in circumstances she could not control and had had no part in creating. I was innocent. Holding my foster records in my hands helped me to witness my own innocence.

It is my firm belief that complete and unfiltered birth information (when known) and medical history (when available) should be on open access to every adopted person whether their adoption is closed or open. Mine was a closed adoption, and I do not advocate for it. An adoptee deserves to know the facts of their earliest life, even if relationships are not built from the foundation of those facts. And, although open adoptions are becoming more common, the level of access to information can vary greatly. Open information in adoption must become the standard across the board. This can help to alleviate so much of the mental and emotional suffering that has plagued the adoptee community for generations. Adoptees should be offered their fullest and unvarnished life history when and if they're ready. Yet, many adoptees still push through their days feeling wounded as they wonder what the truth really is.

Wounded Wonderer

"I feel like a mystery to myself! My whole life seems shrouded in mystery. Keeping me alienated from the facts of my own story makes it very clear that there are people out there who believe I don't matter. That in itself is traumatic, hard, and heartbreaking."

That's how Peter expressed his feelings of being a wounded wonderer. Beyond the many adoption-related challenges he'd faced, the pain of being denied access to truth was his most extreme pain point. "It's a 12 on a scale of 10," he said. "I feel disempowered to fill in the blank pages of my own life."

These blank pages can be very hard on adoptees. Abby tries to work things out even in her dreams. "I have this recurring dream that I'm standing in front of a vault that holds the answers to the questions I've been wondering about all my life as an adoptee. I'm begging the people around me for answers. I'm asking them to unlock the vault of truth. They just stand there and do nothing. It's like they don't even see me. They don't hear my pleas. They hold the power. I hold none."

Adoptees can be made to feel small and disregarded as they wonder who would want to keep another human being locked out of their truth. So many express wanting to shout from the rooftops that they're worthy of seeing the information that is theirs to see. They don't want watered-down truth. Adoptees desire *the* truth.

All too often if adoptees are presented with some outside version of truth, it is modified to be digestible to others. Versions of truth that are easier on others but ultimately harder on the adoptee may sound like: We rescued you. You were just an infant — you can't possibly remember. Your medical history isn't that important, anyway. Your bio mom couldn't take care of you, so she gave you up. Your birth mother loved you so much that she had to let you go. We are your new family now. We don't see color and difference. You must be so grateful to have been adopted.

Countless offhand "comforts" are thrown the adoptee's way and, no matter the good intentions behind them, these words fail to forge foundations of truth, trust, and transparency. In fact, they verge on toxic positivity. These kinds of comments leave the adoptee feeling even more erased, lost, ashamed, and alone. Adoptees are often forced to bypass their pain because others may want to hear only what's comfortable for them.

Take as another example the phrases "adoption means love" and "adoption is love." These words are often used as part of the adoption narrative, most of the time with very good intentions. These phrases are used to express the sense of love present within the adoption triad of bio parent, adoptee, and adoptive parent. They are especially focused on expressing the love that adoptive parents feel for their adopted child. So please stay with me as I share this personal story and how we may want to reconsider the use of these phrases when speaking to or about adoptees.

My adoptive mother recited these phrases to me, over and over, as I grew up. To my mom adoption was love, bottom line. She tried to soothe me with this belief. I used to say these words out loud and to myself — well into my adulthood — in the hopes that I could fully believe them. I even self-published a book, several years ago, containing a compilation of stories from the adoption triad with the title, in part, of "adoption means love." The book held diverse perspectives on and experiences of adoption, yet the title spoke to a narrative I was still struggling with, since I was coming out of the fog myself. I couldn't help but feel like something was missing within those three words.

I began to discover that part of my journey was to flesh out those words and come to a definition of adoption that felt more complete and more representative of my lived experience. The truth was that adoption didn't always feel like love to me — not completely. The experience wasn't that cut-and-dried. Adoption also felt like loss, uncertainty, and isolation. It often felt sad and unfair. There were times when I was deeply homesick for a place I didn't even know. I missed my original people in a way that gutted me. There were many days when I felt desperate and hopeless.

With whom do you share these kinds of feelings when you're adopted? Trying to contextualize all those feelings on your own will drive you close to a place called madness. My adoptive mother didn't know this, but it would have been far kinder, and much more comforting, for her to say, "I'm not here to define adoption for you — I'm not here to tell you what it means — but I am here to support you and to help you honor and speak whatever feels most true to you."

You see, when others tell adoptees that adoption means love or that adoption is love, in essence they are blocking adoptees from arriving at their own definition. Is there love within adoption? The answer can be yes. Yet, so many other emotions are wrapped up in the adoptee experience. Adoption means so many things. The meaning of adoption, for the adoptee, is multilayered and constantly unfolding. The most loving thing we can do is offer adoptees the space to discover, in their own time, what adoption means to them.

I've had several adoptive parents reach out to me recently and share their thoughts on openness and truth as they parent their adopted children. I'd like to share just a few of these comments.

Adoptive parent 1: "We adopted my son through foster care. He has some memories. I have everything I could find in an envelope in a safe-deposit box for when he is older and curious, along with a letter that lets him know I support him and will help him however I can. I answer any questions he has, and we have had a unique chance to be in contact with a bio aunt of his who has been wonderful and can answer a lot of questions that I can't."

Adoptive parent 2: "We encourage our kids to always ask questions, no matter what the questions are! Always come to us, is our message, and we will answer those questions or help find the answers if we don't know them in that moment."

Adoptive parent 3: "We adopted our daughter at birth, and we have always welcomed her questions about her birth family. I wish I could do more for her. I think our openness and our offering of as much truth as we know — not making anything up — is enough for now."

Each of these adoptive parents displays a willingness to be open *with* their child and *for* their child. They display an honoring of truth. This kind of welcome can mean so much to adoptees. It's truly how we begin to forge connection and depth in parent-child relationships and help adoptees feel less wounded as they wonder.

I believe, as adult adoptees, that we can parent ourselves in this way. We can stay open and be honest about our needs as we forge deeper connection with ourselves along the path of self-discovery. We can lovingly and respectfully nurture ourselves as we become more and more aware of what our adoption experience means to us.

MIRROR EXERCISE

Here is a simple exercise that I do every morning, in the mirror, as I begin my day. I hope this exercise – one of self-witnessing – can help you, as it does me, stay open as you seek out truth. I hope it always reminds you to be your own best friend and supporter along the way.

1. Stand in front of a mirror in a power pose. Make sure that your bare feet are firmly planted on the ground, with your legs shoulder width apart. Place one hand over your heart and the other hand on the mirror, with palm pressing in.

2. This pose can help you instantly feel a sense of inner peace, strength, connection, and confidence. Breathe deeply. Exhale completely. Tap your toes gently on the floor to ground your body.

3. On the exhale, look into your eyes reflected in the mirror and say:
   - I stand here *with* me and *for* me.
   - I see myself.
   - I am *safe* to wonder.
   - I stay *open* to the truths that await me.

- I *welcome* deep connection with myself.
- I *care* for my feelings along the way.
- My feelings are *worthy* of care.

I understand that even speaking these words out loud to yourself might be triggering because, as an adoptee, you may have lived years without acknowledging yourself in this way. But by seeing yourself – by honoring your reflection – and speaking these words, you are reminded that you are safe to feel and to wonder. You are reminded that staying open is always better than being closed, and that the opposite of resistance is assistance. When you open a portal to truth, I believe the whole universe conspires on your behalf. It assists you when you no longer resist it.

Take this exercise and all the exercises in this book at your own pace. Please hear me on this: never push yourself beyond what you are ready for. Step-by-step, you will gently move yourself out of those places of self-protection that may be keeping you stuck in the thoughts/behaviors/choices/and situations that no longer serve you.

Once again, I want to repeat just how proud I am of you. I hope you can feel my pride as you read these words because every word I write is infused with love for you. You've started healing the deepest hurts of your adoptee experience. You are finding your way to freedom and to a truth that is yours to claim.

—⟊—

ADOPTEE AWAKENING: *Adoptee stories cannot be wrapped up in a neat and tidy package. It's okay to be honest about the complexity of the adoption experience, even if it's hard for someone else to hear.*

Denial Disrupts the Adoptee's Sense of Inner Peace

I want to take a moment and emphasize how damaging denial can be for adoptees. Denial is the act of declaring something to be untrue. In essence, if an adoptee is denied access to the facts of their earliest story (birth records, foster records, medical records), they're being told that those facts are untrue. If an adoptee is denied their truest identity — that of their first me — then the fullest expression of who adoptees feel they are is being defined as untrue or not even existing. If an adoptee's birth history is denied, then the adoptee is being told that what and who they feel pulsing through their veins isn't real. Denial disrupts an adoptee's sense of inner peace as it disregards what the adopted person innately knows to be true of their life before being adopted.

I can recall an afternoon, many years ago, while visiting my first mother in England. I was eighteen years old and enjoying time outside with her and sharing a moment of one-on-one conversation. I felt delightfully caught up in this sensation of being my mum's daughter. Even as a somewhat emotionally closed-off teen, I remember softening to this feeling and letting it in. It wasn't always easy for me to soften and to allow, yet in that moment I was doing so. It felt peaceful.

That's when a neighbor came into my mum's garden from across the street. She asked my mum, "Well, who do we have here?" Mum looked panicked and stumbled over her words for a moment. Then she said, "This is Michelle. She's a relative from the US."

My heart broke into a million little pieces. I wanted my mum to tell the truth of who I was and of who she was to me. I wanted her to claim me as her daughter, out loud. It was not a claim she was ready to make.

When the neighbor left I asked my mum, "Why didn't you tell her that I'm your daughter?" Mum said, "It's none of her business. I didn't think she needed to know." I looked at my mum with tears in my eyes and said, "It's the truth. I needed to hear you speak the truth."

I felt further erased in that moment and more invisible than I'd ever felt in my life. Instead of the truth, my mum spoke words that were more digestible for both herself and her neighbor. *Relative* was more palatable than *daughter*.

In that moment, I'd been denied being acknowledged as a daughter. Denied of unconditional love, it seemed. It was as if my mum was looking right at me but denying my very existence. I likened myself to that rose my pastor had spoken of when I was thirteen, the rose that was plainly seen yet still denied. I felt like a sin in my mum's eyes; I felt dirty. My mum's need for privacy and secrecy disrupted and disorganized any sense of inner peace that I had opened up to that afternoon. Right before my eyes, my first mother had declared the truth of me as untrue. I died a little on that day. I was my mum's secret, and it appeared that's how I would remain.

—ɷ—

ADOPTEE AWAKENING: *Adoptees are human beings. They are not secrets.*

The Impact of Relinquishment Secrecy

So often adoptees struggle with not feeling seen by others in an authentic way because they know they've been and likely still are someone's secret. People out there know the adoptee was relinquished. Sometimes the relinquishment becomes a family secret. The adoptee may be aware that someone knows something and that they are unwilling to openly share.

As adoptees, we don't always know who this someone is. We don't always know if love and an arms-open embrace await us in that unknown place. We don't know if our dreams of reunion that we hold in our heart of hearts will ever come true. What we do know, instinctively, is that someone out there holds the secret of us, like a heavily guarded hand of cards. Our perception is that they hold the power, and we feel powerless ourselves.

As much as adoptees want and dream of answers to their questions, we often feel the need to protect those holding the cards. Many adoptees share an odd sense of duty to protect strangers — some of whom are bio family members — even if it hurts to be the keeper of the family secret. Adoptees also worry that they might hurt their adoptive family members in the process of illuminating their truth. Here are some comments that I've heard from adoptees on how secrecy impacts their life:

"As an adoptee I struggle with sharing my honest feelings. It's like someone gets hurt when you're honest. So I stay quiet. I stay a secret."

"Honoring myself and speaking my truth seems impossible as an adoptee. Someone always gets hurt when you choose to honor yourself. I don't honor me. I just disappear in all the secrecy."

"People I love get hurt when I choose to acknowledge what's real. I have stopped acknowledging those parts of myself. It's sad. I don't know what else to do but to remain a secret."

As I struggled with the decision of reaching out to my first parents in my teen years, I clearly remember battling with these thoughts: What if my mother and father have children of their own? Is it right for me to want them to know that they have a sister who was left behind? Is it right for me to want to know my own bio siblings? What if one bio parent has a husband or wife who doesn't know about me? What if the truth of me ruins a marriage? What if the knowledge of my presence ruins someone's life? What if I hurt my adoptive family just because I want to honor what I need? These questions can be cruel because they leave the adoptee viewing herself as someone with the capacity to ruin whatever or whomever they touch, just because they hunger to know the truth — just because they exist.

Of all the information that adoptees don't have, they often do know that they're someone's secret. And that's hard. My coaching client Olivia expanded on this: "It's like being in mid-sentence all the time. I don't know who knows what, and so I can't complete the sentence. I'm not sure how to arrive at a place of completeness in my life. I just know that I'm someone's secret, and that makes me feel invisible and sad."

Another of my clients, Lucinda, shares this: "I'm very inquisitive. Not knowing the truth of my story is hard. When you add the thought that I'm also a secret to others, it's a continuation of the hurt. It makes me feel even more unsettled and disempowered inside."

As adopted people, often we want to protect someone so much that we are willing to shrink within their secret shadows so they avoid further hurt. We often identify ourselves as the source of someone else's embarrassment and shame — even if we don't recognize that we're doing so. We can fall into the false belief that we're being selfish for wanting to free ourselves from the bondages of secrecy. We tell ourselves that it's better to do what's best for them and ignore the very thing that we need.

As for myself, I believed that I had no choice but to be part of my first parents' secret world. I wanted to protect them so much that I was willing to stay in their shadows so that they could avoid being outed. Somehow, in my mind, I concluded that being the dutiful keeper of my first parents' secret meant I could forever be their good little girl. Maybe I could even be loved by them.

As I hid in the shadows of my first parents' secret world, I never thought for a moment that I was abandoning myself in the process. That I was hurting myself by becoming smaller and smaller. That I was hurting myself by becoming more and more of a secret.

How small and how secret do we, as adoptees, need to become in order to keep someone else safe from the truth? Over time I realized that I could no longer live as someone's secret. I could no longer tell myself that I didn't need to know. I was no longer willing to deny the truth. I could no longer leave myself behind while others went on living.

Self-abandonment is the most tragic of all abandonments. Self-rejection is the cruelest form of rejection. Adoptees often harbor a strong fear of rejection and abandonment, as I did. We try to stay safe by living in secrecy. What adoptees may not realize is that, in the doing, they are abandoning and rejecting themselves. They are abandoning their truth and denying themselves a life of being seen, heard, and known.

As long as adoptees hide in the cave of someone else's secrecy, they will remain a mystery to themselves. Adoptees do not deserve this kind of existence. They should never be required to bear the heavy burden of relinquishment secrecy. They never signed up for that.

I still vividly remember the day I took action toward stepping away from relinquishment secrecy. I was in my late twenties when I walked into my local courthouse and filed a petition to change my last name to Madrid — that of my bio paternal side. Then I placed a public notice on the announcement board. I walked out of that courthouse feeling more freedom than I'd ever felt in my life. It was my first step to becoming *known*.

I'm not saying that every adoptee needs to legally change their name. This was the right move for me; however, it's not for everyone. Neither is tattooing an original first name on an arm. These steps have been helpful for me in illuminating and claiming the truth for myself. Each adoptee will have their unique ways of moving from secrecy to brilliant clarity. No matter what that looks like for you, I want to remind you that nothing is more empowering than a life of clarity and truth, and the deepest place of clarity and truth resides within. It's a place where you can clearly see without even opening your eyes.

A Birth Certificate and a Blank Space

I recently obtained my original birth certificate from the United Kingdom. This document was not included in the foster records that I had received. In all my years, I'd never seen my original birth certificate; I'd only seen my adoption certificate. When the birth certificate arrived to my home in America, I had to take a moment to process. I knew from what others had told me over the years that my first father's name was not listed on the document, but to hold that original birth certificate in my hand — minus the name of my father — was a tough pill to swallow. I didn't even have a surname listed, just my first and middle original name, Julié Dawn.

I felt triggered in that moment, seeing a simple blank line in the space where my father's name should have been listed. So often that's what we get as adoptees — blank spaces where pertinent life information should be. Although I know my birth father's name, it still weighs on my heart that he wasn't included on the piece of paper that documents the life he helped create.

There are certain answers that we, as adoptees, may not receive. We may never have the name of our bio father listed on our birth certificate. In addition, adoptees may not be offered the answers they hope for from a first parent. They may never receive the family medical history they desire. They may not hear others speak answers that feel true to them. It is vital that adoptees begin to shift from a mindset of *not knowing* to one of *knowing*. To begin, adoptees can ask themselves this question: *What is it that I do know?* For the answer to that question, every adoptee must travel within.

Are you ready for a clarity and a truth that cannot be provided on any document or within any file? Are you ready for a truth that no one can take away from you, even if they deny or resist your existence? Are you ready for a truth that will guide you like the North Star for the rest of your life? If so, let's continue on to this chapter's reframing exercise. In chapter 3, you opened the portal to truth, and now in this chapter, through a practice called adoptee priming, you'll feel the energy of your truth opening you to new insights and clarity.

To begin, let's focus in on a belief that I adhere to: peace starts with the transfer of power from "them" to "me." When we shift the power structure from the outside world to the inner, we begin to hear our own truths emerge. External chatter is quieted. We disassociate from anything outside our internal knowing. In other words, when we look to outside forces as the only way toward truth, we do ourselves a great disservice as adoptees. We lessen our power. Here's what I've grown to understand: our ultimate power — and, yes, peace — is found in a sacred and divine place within us. Our purest truth is found within ourselves, too.

Here are a few opening questions I'd like you to consider as we move into our reframing exercise:

1. As an adoptee, will you extinguish the truth of your existence, or are you willing to excavate that truth?
2. Will you extinguish the truth of your voice, or are you willing to excavate that truth?
3. Will you extinguish the truth of your identity, or are you willing to excavate that truth?

You see, we have a choice as adopted people, the choice to extinguish our truth as we rely on outside sources to define us and fill in those blank pages of our lives or the choice to excavate our truth from the deepest places within ourselves — a place where *the* truth awaits us and longs to fill the void with never-ending love. I have personally witnessed adoptees doing the brave work of soulful excavation. I have seen them travel, both externally and internally, to places once unknown in order to excavate the truth and gain clarity.

Remember Peter from earlier in the chapter? He shared with me that pain point number 3, the pain of being denied access to truth, was the most difficult for him. "It's a 12 on a scale of 10," he said. "I feel disempowered to fill in the blank spaces of my own life."

I guided Peter through this reframing exercise, and it greatly reduced his pain from a 12 to a 6. He now does this exercise daily to connect himself to a deeper sense of truth and power.

Adoptee Priming

Priming is an exercise that supports you in filtering out negative stimuli so you can prime yourself toward a life that feels ignited and empowered. I first learned of priming while attending an event led by world-renowned life strategist Tony Robbins. I have modified this practice to support adoptees in the accessing of their truth. One goal of this practice is to remind adoptees that they are the creators of their lives, not the managers of their circumstances.

Take that thought in for a moment as it relates to the feeling adoptees often have of being denied access to the truth of their earliest life and origins. We have a decision to make as adoptees: Will we focus on the lack of information or the misinformation from external sources, or will we focus on the wealth of information from our internal source?

Priming supports you in adjusting your thoughts and emotions through movement, breath, and visualization, helping you decide what to focus on in your life. The fact is, our problems and our wounds, as adopted people, are calling us to a higher level. They're calling us to be greater! I truly believe this, and I live this belief each and every day. This practice of adoptee priming, for me, has been pivotal. It has helped me filter out negative stimuli so that I can focus on the truth of who I am and all I'm here to be. Priming can do that for you, too.

The Gratitude Grab

This adoptee priming exercise will ask you to move into a place of gratitude through a technique I call the Gratitude Grab. Practicing gratitude is an act of truth telling. When we are in a state of gratitude, we open ourselves up, lay down our protective mechanisms, and tell it like it is. We experience an expansive truth. Within a space of gratitude, we can acknowledge the harder moments of life but still feel the miraculous pulse of living.

Here I want to make clear that experiencing gratitude is very different from being told to "just be grateful." "Just be grateful," to me, means that we as adoptees are supposed to say "thank you." That's very difficult for adoptees as they wrestle with the narrative of adoption. Being asked to say "I'm grateful" and "thank you" in the face of unresolved loss and grief can feel highly dismissive, like a damaging expectation from the outside world. In essence, adoptees are being asked to mute their grief — to be grateful and not grieving. "Just be grateful" doesn't offer the space for both.

Gratitude, however, is a state of being. It holds no promise of an outcome. I can experience gratitude in my heart for my life and all those I love and still be offered the space to grieve what's been lost. For me, that's the difference. Gratitude offers inclusiveness, something all adoptees long for. It's the *both/and* of the adoptee experience. Not a day goes by when I don't pray for the *both/and* to be more fully embraced by the adoption conversation. Gratitude offers the opportunity to feel the totality of our truth and of our lived experience as adoptees.

A Prayer to Self

I'd like to initiate the following exercise (we're almost there!) with a prayer to yourself. The adoptee community is a diverse one that spans the globe. Regardless of your spiritual beliefs and practices, please allow yourself to say these words of opening prayer with me. We have been created, as adoptees, by a wonderful and loving Source — whether you pray to God, Buddha, Muhammad, the angels, your spirit guides, life, or the Universe. Your self is part of this creation.

I understand that the challenging moments of the adoptee experience can make us question the divine within us. We can find ourselves questioning if the divine even sees us. I've been there, I know. Yet I also know that speaking into this place of self is a transformational practice connecting us to an ever-present energy of love and peace. It would be impossible to go inward to this place of all-knowing self — to the love and light within us — without emerging anew, even in some small way.

Here is my opening prayer for you. If you feel comfortable — and there is no pressure at all — please put both hands over your heart as you read these words with me:

> In this moment, I open and welcome the wisdom of divine self to speak. I ask that inner peace and knowing support me at this time. I release any and all resistance to what I'm here to discover. I welcome the transfer of personal power from outer world to inner world. May all the parts within me feel connected, loved, and accepted. May the purest truth — that which can come only from within me — lead me forward from this day on.

You may speak this whole prayer or just parts. You can even write your own prayer if you feel inspired to do so. Connect to what feels good and right for you. Please know that this prayer is here to support you as you visualize the key to opening up that place of truth-filled power within. It's the place that self knows well. It *is* self. Each time we go to self in prayer, we strengthen our connection to the divine within us. This prayer offers you a moment of centering and calm as you connect to your beautiful and empowering truth.

REFRAMING EXERCISE
Adoptee Priming: Accessing Personal Power and Truth

Sit comfortably in a chair, feet centered and flat on the ground. Your back should be straight. There should be nothing in your lap.

Breathe

- We will start with a breathing sequence: three sets of ten breaths will be the repetition as you breathe in and out through your nose.
- Close your eyes, and as you breathe in and out through your nose, your arms will move up and down with the rhythm of your breath, as you extend your arms up to the sky and then down to your shoulders.
- Begin your three sets of ten breaths through your nose, with arms in unison, now.
- When you have completed the three sets, stop and place your hands in your lap, with palms up.
- Notice what you feel. Do you feel a tingling sensation anywhere in your body? Do you feel relaxed? Do you feel a sense of peace? Just feel into this moment.

Practice the Gratitude Grab

- This is the *both/and* of the adoptee priming experience. Remember, as I said earlier, you can experience gratitude in your heart for your life and all those you love and still be offered the space to access and acknowledge what's been lost. You are safe to explore the totality of your truths within a space of gratitude.

- Now grab hold of three moments of gratitude. With eyes closed and palms up, resting in your lap, envision three moments in your life that you can have gratitude for. These can be little moments or big moments, harder moments or easier moments, current moments or past moments. One at a time, relive those three moments.

- Feel the beauty. Feel the joy. Feel the gratitude. Feel the moment.

- See what you saw then. Hear what you heard then. Feel what you are feeling. What did you learn?

- Let that inner smile come through. Let those tears come through. Let it all come through you. Whatever you feel, let it flow.

- Experience each of your three moments of gratitude as if you are there, right now.

- If your mind wonders, that's okay. Just come back to the feeling of gratitude with these words: *I am safe to feel gratitude in this moment. I am safe to explore my truth.*

Share the Light

- Now breathe normally and imagine that you are taking in a white light, a gold light, or a blue light. See the light coming into the crown of your head from the Universe.

- See the light cleansing, washing, and healing your mind, body, and emotions.
- Feel the light filling up those blank pages, blank lines, and missing pieces of your adoptee journey.
- Bathe in the light. Let your hands and arms follow as the light moves down through your body and then back up with a surge of energy as you release it back into the sky. Repeat this flow of light energy.
- Let this energy make the unknown parts of you known. Let the energy make you feel more alive, more full of joy, and more full of love.
- Let the energy strengthen the best parts of you. The real you. The true you. The truth of you that no document can hold or no file can form. The you that holds the key to all that is true. Connect with that person as you continue to breathe. See yourself holding the key to your truth. Stay with this feeling for a moment longer.

Celebrate

- Ask yourself, *What are three illuminating truths that have arrived to me in this adoptee priming?* I like to start with three because I believe in the power of Three to Thrive (the practice of choosing three things to make happen each day).
- Connect with your first truth. Step into it and see yourself there. Celebrate it. You're coming into alignment with your truth, and that's a beautiful victory.
- Embody your truth. What does that feel like? Feel it! What does that look like? See it!

- Connect with your second truth now. Step into it and experience it fully. You're not asking for the truth from an outside source anymore. No, that's done. You are claiming your truth. A truth that no one and nothing can take from you. Celebrate that!
- Connect with your third truth now. See the impact of claiming this truth. Feel the gratitude of no longer living a life of not knowing, a life spent feeling denied of truth. You're now embracing the purest form of truth – that which is found within.
- Everything you need to know about the truth of who you are is found within you, right here and now. No human being out there can give you this kind of truth.
- Now, bring your truths into your heart space. Feel those truths connecting to all that you hold gratitude for. Let these truths awaken in your heart.

Open your eyes and start to feel the energy within you building up. Feel the love, the joy, the excitement, and the energy of your life. Bring it all into your heart, and breathe it in. Own it. This is your true nature. This is you no longer tethered to the thoughts of not knowing or being denied truth. This is you living free. Make the sound of what freedom feels like to you. Go ahead, I want to hear you! Now take a deep breath in and exhale. Extend your arms in front of you, and then wrap them around yourself and give yourself a kind and loving hug.

When you are ready, you can journal on the following questions and connect with the empowering truths that come to you:

- What if you always had the power to access your truth?
- What if even the pain and problems within this adoptee experience were gifts?

- What if the truths within you guided you deeper toward meaning and toward freedom of pain?
- What if every moment along this adoptee journey has happened *for* you and not *to* you? How would that change your life?
- What if today becomes more compelling than yesterday's challenges?
- What if tomorrow will be magnificent because you've begun this practice of priming, along with grabbing hold of gratitude?

Respect and honor your truths. I cannot say this enough! Dedicate yourself to priming and grabbing hold of gratitude, daily. It takes only ten to fifteen minutes and can completely transform how you step into your day and deal with the challenging thoughts, emotions, and situations that can arise. I'm so proud of you. As you continue to practice adoptee priming, more truths will come to you. I can't wait to hear how these inner truths redirect and renew your life.

As we move forward to chapter 5, we'll look at the words that can harm adoptees and the words that can help heal them. I'll guide you through a simple yet effective exercise of embracing healing words and thoughts that help shift limited thinking into limitless believing. We'll work to shed the labels that can keep adoptees stuck in a place of limit and lack.

Adoptee Affirmation

I can access my truth at any time.
Real truth lives inside me.
I trust in this source of power within.

Chapter Five

A Sticky Residue

The Pain of Familial Rejection and Words That Harm

Here's something I've learned as an adoptee: the sticky residue of familial rejection can negatively impact our sense of self-worth. Familial rejection, typically parental rejection, can be experienced in the family of origin or in the adoptive family. The fallout of feeling left, whether physically or emotionally, can adhere to an adoptee's spirit if not safely addressed and healed.

This sticky residue can ultimately result in other types of rejection fears like those of social rejection, relationship rejection, and romantic rejection. When a child sees himself as rejected by their parents of origin or their adoptive parents, that can deeply impact that child's sense of self-value and self-confidence as they grow. Here I want to note that not everyone who has relinquished the role of parenting a child has neglected or abused that child. Sometimes bio parents are simply not prepared or are too young to offer their best to their child. It's also important to state that not all adoptive parents are equipped to raise their adoptive children, either. My adoptive father's struggle with alcohol addiction rendered him incapable of being present for me. My first parents didn't abuse me, yet their decision to relinquish me left me feeling hopelessly abandoned and unloved for years. There was a lingering feeling of being rejected by both sides. The impact of familial rejection can leave adoptees struggling with their sense of identity, too. When you don't know who you are — when you feel void of identity and worth — someone else will define your identity and your value for you, even if their definition hurts and diminishes you.

In 2019 I was in London with my family. We were visiting a museum and looking at an art display on the plight of orphaned children from the 1700s. Part of the display was of children's white button-down shirts hanging on individual hooks. On each shirt collar was a label with words that had been spoken to these orphaned children by their caretakers, words like: *You won't ever be anything. You are not a little girl anymore. It's all your fault, as usual. Your mother's not capable of looking after you. You're a liar. Don't bother trying.*

I remember standing there reading the words on those little shirts. I thought about the weight of those words on the innocent children. I thought about how confused and lost those children must have felt. Then I reflected on the words in my own foster records from the United Kingdom, words like: *Unwanted. Illegitimate. Strange-looking. Dark. Difficult to place.* And my heart broke for all children who are spoken to or about in ways that dim their light. These children often grow into adults who still carry the heavy weight of those words — words that can become their logos of limitation.

Logos of Limitation

Logos of limitation are the labels that imprint limiting beliefs on an adoptee's spirit and negatively shape how they see themselves and the world around them. One example of this would be the framing of adoption as a "second-best" option, which, intended or not, labels adoptees as "second-choice kids" — a choice made after having biological children has been unsuccessful. These limiting labels can claw their way deep into the adoptee psyche. What could be more insensitive than suggesting to another human being that they're second best? Yet this has been happening for decades. Perhaps you can understand why the comment "You were chosen" can be such a tough one for adoptees. Inside our heads we hear, "Chosen, but as a second choice."

Here's how Caroline explains her experience with the logos of limitation: "As a child, rejection and the words spoken about being rejected stayed with me. It sucks that careless words can stick to you like that. I don't know how to change it. I always hear, inside my head, that I'm unwanted, too opinionated, unloved! I try to talk myself out of it, but the proof is there. If I wasn't these things, then why would my first parents have left?"

Pain point number 4, the pain of familial rejection, weaves a wicked, sticky web. Caroline was feeling the pain on a strong level: a 9.5 on a scale of 10. I'll share more of Caroline's story later in this chapter, but it's safe to say that her own beliefs of rejection and abandonment, along with the judgmental words and comments pinned on her by her adoptive dad about being too assertive with her words and opinions, had created logos of limitation that seemed impossible to shift.

I have been asked countless times if familial rejection can be felt as both first family rejection and as adoptive family rejection. Let me stress here that the answer is yes. As I shared earlier, I have experienced this pain point on both sides of my biology and biography. To be totally transparent, the pain point of familial rejection has been one of my greatest struggles. I have, without a doubt, been a solid 10 on the scale.

I struggled with familial rejection on two levels: rejection by my parents of origin and the chronic emotional rejection that existed in my adoptive home. I was highly sensitive and, on most days, in the crossfire of arguments between my alcohol-dependent father and my codependent mother. I had nowhere to go to safely express my feelings, fears, insecurities, and confusion. The words my adoptive father used toward me were like sharp blades cutting through my spirit. With a single word, Dad could reduce me to dust. Life inside my adoptive home was explosive and exhausting.

My dad's anger would rise and would be focused on me. In his Jack Daniels–impaired state, he would find me and begin picking on my appearance, often calling me a "hair lip" because I had dark, tiny, yet visible, hairs on my upper lip. My dad also called me an "A-rab." It was the way he said the word — with such disdain — that left me in tears. I began to hate the way I looked: my dark, thick, wavy hair; my thick eyebrows; my deep-brown eyes; and my skin that, in the summer, became "dark as a blackberry," as my adoptive aunts would often comment. I was an exotic-looking child, and that further alienated me from everyone around me in my adoptive world.

Words and thoughts of self-condemnation became a daily practice. What I longed for was to be adored by my father. It felt as if I repulsed him. Mom would try to explain my dad's anger away by saying he had "a short fuse." I couldn't understand where his frustrations originated or how to make them go away. I do remember feeling a great sense of relief when he was out of the house, along with a deep sense of guilt over having that feeling.

I never questioned the words being used toward me by my father. I never thought for one minute that they weren't true. After all, my mother never suggested otherwise. In addition, Dad's words seemed, on some level, to reflect the words used about me in foster care in the United Kingdom. I was "dark and strange-looking." I was "difficult to place." *This must be why my first parents left and why my adoptive father drinks.* Word by word, I pinned all the limiting labels onto my young spirit. Those labels became my story. Day by day, I felt more and more worthless — more and more responsible for the rejection.

The only place I knew to find a sense of peace and a glimpse of what joy might feel like was on my beloved bicycle. I used to ride with my best friend in fourth grade, a girl named Regina. I would have done anything to be like her. She had long blonde hair tied back in ribbons. A Southern belle, Regina had a knack for stringing two-syllable words out into three syllables, or more — sentences oozed from her mouth like sweet molasses.

While bike riding on a warm Saturday afternoon, in northern Mississippi, Regina and I decided to park along a dusty road. We put our kickstands down and made a plan to pick flowers and put them in the baskets attached to our bikes. My basket was white with yellow and pink flowers on the front, the perfect accessory for a bicycle I adored. I stood admiring my bike, as I did on most sunny afternoons. I was holding bright wildflowers in my hand and thinking about the power I felt when I pedaled fast, pretending that I was Wonder Woman on some grand mission.

That's when Regina posed her question to me: "Michelle, are you a bastard?" I just stood there with my eyes solidly fixed on my friend. I wanted to jump on my bike and flee, flying up-up-and-away like my favorite superhero in her invisible plane. I couldn't move, though. I stood there frozen and unable even to flinch. Bending down to pick her flowers, Regina pressed on, emphasizing the word that I despised.

"I said, are you a bastard? I don't even know what that means, but it sounds really bad. My mom says it has something to do with your real parents not wanting you and giving you away." Plucking a bouquet of wildflowers from the dirt, Regina turned to me and in the same breath asked, "Aren't these pretty?" I looked at her flowers and commented that they were indeed pretty. I prayed that the other part of her question would simply vanish into thin air. It did. For Regina, that is.

I hated the word *bastard*. More than the word itself, I hated how it sounded when another person said it. Yes, I had heard the word before — too many times to count — from my dad and from the adults around me who used the word casually as they referred to kids like me. I didn't have to fully know the meaning to understand the dishonor attached to it. After Regina's brutally direct line of questioning, I said to myself: *Enough is enough ... I'm going to find out exactly what this word means.*

As a curious and probing child, I went straight home and looked up the word in my dictionary. Thumbing through the pages I found it, right in front of me in black and white. *Bastard:* (1) Noun meaning: illegitimate child. (2) Adjective meaning: impure, irregular, imperfect, inferior.

I sat on the couch for a long time that afternoon, the dictionary planted in the middle of my lap. "This is who I am," I said out loud. I felt flustered and guilt-ridden. The heat of humiliation burned my cheeks. I peered out the window behind me and saw that my wildflowers were wilting in my bike basket. They had stood so much taller earlier in the day, but then so had I. In that moment I took Regina's words and pushed them so deep inside myself that they became a part of me: I was a bastard.

I felt so much smaller than Regina. It was a feeling that I couldn't rid myself of. After all, my first parents left me. Regina's first parents stayed. Something wasn't right. Something didn't make sense. Something was wrong. *Maybe sometimes children are just born unwanted. Maybe some kids are born impure and inferior. Maybe I'm just one of those unlucky kids.* Lucky kids aren't rejected by their first parents. Lucky kids aren't called bastards. A lucky kid doesn't stand out as someone who doesn't belong, someone who doesn't quite fit into the family she's been given.

I didn't ride my bike with Regina after that day. I was too scared that she might ask me the question again. I was afraid that I'd be forced to answer her. I was ashamed that the answer to her question was, "Yes, Regina, I am a bastard." I didn't know how I could ever feel safe again in Regina's presence. I felt alienated just by the thought of her. I loved my friend, but I had learned how to put up walls in order to protect my young heart. The walls went up that afternoon, and they didn't come down.

I was covered in the sticky residue of rejection left behind by my first parents. I was becoming wrapped up in logos of limitation. Still, I felt required to put on the appearance of a girl overjoyed to be adopted. Only, I wasn't. Most of the time, adoption didn't feel joyful. Adoption hurt. Alcoholism hurt, too. Being adopted was a constant reminder that someone somewhere had left. It was also a reminder that, even though the wider adoption narrative can focus on the flaws of the bio family, adoptive families have flaws, too. Where do you turn to talk about that?

The word *bastard* became a part of my identity. It was the theme of my story. *Impure. Inferior. Unwanted. Unloved. Unacceptable.* The words kept stacking up in my head. Words that drowned out the sounds of any truth held in my heart. To me it's no coincidence that the words *story* and *store* are only one letter apart. The story we tell ourselves (where we place our focus) becomes the reality we store inside and live out in our daily lives. All too often, adoptees hear words and stories that harm. The foundation of their earliest thought patterns are often built on harmful words.

One of the most powerful lessons I've learned is this: words can harm or words can heal. Words can refute or words can affirm. There really is no in between. As I shared earlier in this book, words create thoughts and thoughts create our beliefs and the reality we live. It's like that childhood saying, You are what you eat. If I was told this saying once, I was told it a thousand times while growing up.

The same sentiment holds true for the words and thoughts we consume — they become who we are. For example, if you tell yourself that you're unwanted, then you will likely feel unwanted in most or all situations and relationships. Your story — the belief playing on repeat — is that you are unwanted. It's where your focus is going and, as we've discussed, focus creates energy. Where focus goes, energy flows.

The sharp pain of familial rejection and abandonment runs deep. It carves deep and wide caverns of loss through the adoptee's spirit. Adoptees may see themselves as irreversibly broken. What other explanation would cause first parents to leave their child and sometimes cause adoptive parents to turn away? All too often, adoptees hold this question deep within themselves. They bottle the question up, along with all the pain that comes with it. They live with the sticky residue of rejection and the logos of limitation born of that experience.

—⟋⟍⟍—

ADOPTEE AWAKENING: *As adoptees, we must be able to look at how the sticky residue of familial rejection may be showing up in our lives. Otherwise, rejection's residue can be unknowingly passed down and felt for generations to come.*

I have a coaching client, Florence, whose beloved grandmother was an adoptee. Florence, a nonadoptee, came to me wanting support since she'd grown up aware of her grandmother's lonely struggle with her adoption and the rejection she felt. "My grandmother told me that she didn't feel worthy of living a lot of the time. She carried that feeling around with her all her life. She didn't really love herself. She didn't have anyone to teach her what it meant to love herself, unconditionally, and to be unapologetically real. She didn't know how to use her voice. This has created a sadness inside me because I couldn't help her heal. She's gone now, and I never could offer her the support she so deserved. I'm having a hard time dealing with that."

I've shared my belief that healing is ancestral work. Florence's story is an example of what it looks like when we don't help adoptees heal the pain points that are so real for them. The pain filters down through the generations. As I write these words, I think of all the adoptees who have come before me. My heart is heavy with the thought that so many never received the compassionate care they were worthy of receiving. I hope this book can help to end that unkind cycle and that this sharing of a kinder way forward can help reach those adoptees who feel isolated and alone. I hope my words help adoptees to see the greatness within them and to speak greatness into their lives.

Caroline Speaks Greatness

Speaking greatness into her life is exactly what I worked on with Caroline, who you met earlier in the chapter. I wanted to help Caroline see and speak greatness into all aspects of her life. As a reminder, Caroline was feeling the pain of rejection and words that harm to a high degree: a 9.5 on a scale of 10.

An incredible mother and executive, Caroline felt deeply distraught when she reached out to me for coaching. "I can be in a boardroom and leading a meeting, but inside my head all I hear is that I'm doing something wrong for voicing my opinions and expressing my views. Furthermore, I feel like I don't belong there. Like I'm an impostor trying not to be found out."

I asked Caroline to share with me when she first remembered feeling "wrong" for using her voice and expressing her opinions. She lowered her head and began fidgeting. Then she told me that her adoptive father used to tell her that she was overly opinionated and that this was a bad trait. She began to wonder if this trait was why her first parents had left her.

Caroline feared disappointing her adoptive father, and so she began to hide her opinions. Now every time she's in a setting where she has an opinion to express, Caroline gets knots in her stomach and her throat tightens up. The voice in her head says: "Don't be so opinionated. You're going to blow it all. You know how your assertiveness disappoints your dad. You're going to disappoint everyone here, too."

Caroline told me that her constant limiting logo — the one that plays on repeat in her head — is that she's overly opinionated and too assertive. When I asked her to go deeper than that limiting logo and to excavate the story that's underneath it, she said: "When I assert my voice, I'm being a bad adopted daughter. And my job has always been to be a good one." The threat of another familial rejection seemed credible to Caroline. Her fear was that if she's seen as a bad adopted daughter, she won't be loved and accepted by her father. I wonder if, as we strive to be "good adoptees," we distance ourselves from being "real adoptees," real people with unique thoughts and opinions and a whole lot of wisdom and love to share.

I look back on my own life and the many times I have allowed the limiting thought of "I have nothing of value to say" take over and silence me. I know just how emotionally crippling it is when the false evidence — the logos of limitation — appears so real. I understand the deep despair when, inside your head, you question your own opinions and perspectives because you fear that you'll disappoint and lose love if you voice those things. I have grown to understand, in my own experience, that these feelings reach way back to a time when I felt helpless and alone.

As adoptees, we can unknowingly let the disempowering words and thoughts of condemnation take over. To create some sense of safety, many adoptees disconnect from their ability to speak greatness into their own lives. I've done it! I hold a great deal of compassion for that version of myself because I was just trying to keep my inner child — my first me — safe. I remind myself now that this child is in the most loving hands — the hands of the woman she has grown to be. There is no one who wants my inner child to feel healthy and whole more than I do. I urge adoptees to consider that no one is more qualified to care for their inner child than they are. It's okay to recognize the need for healing and to choose the approaches that work best for you.

I'd like to offer you one approach that you can rely on to shift any word and thought patterns from ones of condemnation to ones of confirmation. The following reframing exercise is a simple and effective anchor to grab hold of. It can reconnect you to your authority to choose your own empowering words and thoughts.

REFRAMING EXERCISE
Change the Channel

The Change the Channel exercise helps adoptees recognize a word or thought of condemnation and stop the downward-spiraling response that can take over and shut them down. It offers the opportunity, in that moment, to shift from words and thoughts of condemnation to ones of confirmation through changing the channel. Think about this: if you're watching the television and a show comes on that you don't want to view, do you stay on that channel or do you change it to a program that you like better? Most of us quickly pick up our remotes and change the channel.

We can do that with our words and thoughts, too. We can use this exercise as our mental remote control to change the channel on the disempowering program showing up in our minds. If we, as adoptees, are not able to catch ourselves in moments when words and thoughts of condemnation are taking over, then we will be prone to keep repeating damaging beliefs and behaviors that do not serve our greater good. It's such a relief to say, "Oh, I'm noticing that I have a disempowering program on inside my head. I'm not this program. I'm not this thought. I'm the one who is witnessing it – I'm the viewer of the thought – and I have the power to change the channel."

Step 1: Stop and notice the word or thought of condemnation. Tap yourself gently on the top of the head, breathe deeply, and drop down into your heart space. Remember, disempowering thoughts reside in the head. Truth lives in the heart. You can ask yourself how that limiting word or thought makes you feel. Get clear on that feeling.

Step 2: Recognize the condemning word or thought. Without judgment, witness it. Understand that you are not the condemning word or thought. You are the one looking at it; you are not it.

Step 3: Forgive the condemning word or thought. You can say, "I forgive this condemning word or thought, this disempowering program. I also forgive myself because I am merely on the wrong channel in my mind. I hold gratitude that I have the power to change the channel and choose better-feeling words and thoughts."

Step 4: Change the channel and choose a word or thought of confirmation. Let your heart speak because it holds the words and thoughts of love and light. Listen for what your heart wants to bring forth. Tune in to that channel! Don't question your heart. Once you've received the better-feeling word or thought, write it down. I like to write down the word or thought of condemnation in my journal, cross it out, and then write the new word or thought of confirmation. It's a transformational practice.

I have used this exercise with youths who have matured out of foster care. In our sessions, they have written down words of condemnation they've experienced, whether they be words of self-condemnation or words of condemnation spoken to them by others. They've written down the negative thoughts that have limited their ability to fully live and love. Then they have changed the channel to new, empowering words and thoughts of confirmation. The shift in their identity and sense of worth has been immediate and absolutely life-changing through just this one anchoring exercise.

As adoptees and as foster youth, we can feel so deeply disempowered by the experiences of removal, relinquishment, and displacement. We lose sight of the voice we possess when so much of our life is directed by the decisions, judgments, and labels of others. The residue of rejection sticks to us. Peeling off the residue takes commitment and a desire to see all the potential we possess. We don't have to take a back seat in our lives anymore. We can take on a front-seat mindset. We have the power to steer our way forward.

I worked with Caroline on her words and thoughts of condemnation through this Change the Channel exercise. She saw herself as too opinionated and too assertive, a judgment originally placed on her by her adoptive father. Through this exercise, she chose healthier thoughts such as "my voice is important" and "what I have to say is important." The truth that Caroline's heart spoke to her was that she is safe to speak her views without risking the loss of love. Loving herself enough to assert her opinions with elegance and grace became her front-seat mindset and greatly reduced her pain. It also gave her the confidence to speak to her father, openly and honestly. Their relationship has been transformed.

I hope the Change the Channel exercise supports you in moments when you feel words and thoughts taking over that don't uplift you. In that moment, pause and say: I can change the channel. Then move through this simple yet effective exercise: stop, recognize, forgive, choose. As we reframe our thoughts and our words, we choose what is confirming and empowering for us. We begin to heal — little by little — those places within that are still covered in the sticky residue of rejection and that still feel the words that have harmed us. As we move toward what is true for us as adoptees, we let go of the logos of limitation and all the words and thoughts of condemnation that helped to create those logos. We can free ourselves from the web of worry, self-doubt, self-condemnation, and the feeling of being impostors. The only proof we need of our worth is found inside us. We only need to seek the wisdom found within.

I have changed the channel on the limiting label from childhood that said I was a bastard. I'm no longer haunted by that word. I know who I am. I'm a legitimate light in this world — wanted and loved — and I make no apology for shining. I decide who I am, and understanding this has opened wide the doors of my heart.

In chapter 6 we'll explore pain point number 5, the pain of distrust. Together we'll look at how this pain point is often unconscious and stems from the fallout of abandonment. Through answering questions and doing a reframing exercise, we'll work to arrive at a place of conscious recognition of where distrust may be showing up and causing trust turbulence in our lives.

Adoptee Affirmation

> Now I am the voice.
> I will lead, not follow.
> I am an adoptee with purpose.
> I choose my words and my thoughts.

Chapter Six

Navigating Trust Turbulence

The Pain of Distrust

As human beings, we have an innate need to trust. It's in our DNA. And the first person we trust is our first mother. We depend on her to provide for our basic needs. The early separation of a child from her mother can often cause trust issues later in life for the child. For adoptees, it's hard to trust when you feel that your basic and primal need for maternal love and protection has been rejected or denied.

If you were to dig down deep into an adoptee's internal world, you'd likely find an innocent soul struggling with the question, *How can I trust anyone when the one I should have been able to trust left?* This question represents the adoptee's (1) perception of trust — their overall understanding of what trust is to them, (2) their belief about trust — the thoughts they continually have about trust, and (3) the data they store in their mind — the evidence of how trust has been broken in their life, which leads to distrust. Fears that represent a fundamental lack of trust may look like fear of intimacy, fear of vulnerability, fear of emotional connection, and fear of being left. These are some of the real and present fears that stem from pain point number 5.

Distrust is an unconscious feeling that causes a sense of disease for the adopted person. It can find the adoptee constantly second-guessing themselves or being afraid of making a mistake. By definition, distrust means to have no trust or confidence in something or someone. I believe that distrust is rooted in self-protection and centered on self-preservation — the adoptee's survival system. The pain of distrust results in a great deal of emotional turbulence for many adoptees. Rejection and abandonment appear as ironclad proof that trusting is a losing game, even a dangerous one.

Trusting seems extremely risky for adoptees who may still be struggling with the fallout of abandonment. It's no wonder that they may also struggle with placing their trust in people. For the adoptee still dealing with abandonment issues, everyone appears untrustworthy.

For me, the turbulence of distrust rumbled through my life for a very long time. I lived disconnected from people because I didn't trust them. I numbed myself from feeling. I told myself, *If I don't feel it, I can't be hurt by it when it all goes away.* Notice that I didn't say, "If it goes away," I said, "When it goes away." I fully expected the people and situations in my life to disappear at one point or another. I spent my days waiting for the big vanishing act. It's where I kept my focus. Often, I would leave romantic relationships before I could be left. This action of leaving first was my self-protection mechanism — my survival system — shifted into high gear.

I viewed everything in my life through the lens of impermanence. Commitment, I believed, was a naive concept. My entire frame of reference was centered on what I perceived to be a failure of commitment by my first parents. So I didn't fully invest myself emotionally in any relationship. Why would I? How could I when my own first parents had broken the primal bonds of devotion to me, their child? I held an unyielding mistrust of everyone. I didn't even trust myself. It was hard to trust myself when I didn't know what I may have done to cause my first mother and father to leave. I felt guilty and ashamed, but I didn't know why.

Guilt and Shame

Guilt and shame both originate from the outside in. Guilt is a learned social emotion that may cause the adopted person to continually have thoughts like: *It's all my fault, I'm a mistake, and I'm not wanted*. The adoptee may feel deserving of blame for some imaginary offense, or they may feel a deep and painful sense of inadequacy. Shame comes from the negative reflections of others. It lives in the mind and body, causing, in many cases, high levels of disease. Shame is a painful condition of feeling disgraced and buried in shortcomings.

Both guilt and shame damage the adoptee's sense of identity, molding who they believe they are and who they believe they are not. Guilt and shame can also frame what adoptees believe they can and can't become. When the adoptee feels guilty, ashamed, and uncertain about their own sense of identity, trusting anyone or anything seems close to impossible.

Yet, as mentioned earlier, the desire to trust is in our DNA, as adoptees and as human beings. We want to trust others. We want to trust ourselves. I held an innate longing to trust, even through all the doubt and instability that I experienced growing up. The adoptees I coach today do, too. I often hear words like this coming from them: "I want to trust my decisions. I want to trust others. I want to trust myself. I don't know how to trust."

Losing first parents is bound to bring about lifelong struggles and ongoing challenges. It can never be assumed that the adoptee has "moved on" from the great loss they have experienced. The assumption that it should be easy for adoptees to simply forget about what and who came before their adoption has caused an immense amount of pain and suffering in our community.

As both an adoptee and an adoptive parent, I know how vitally important it is for adoptive parents to show up for their children and consistently offer them unconditional love, unending support, and compassionate care. I also understand just how important it is, as an adult adoptee, to offer myself the same kind of love, support, and care. When adoptees do not receive that kind of support, their distrust of other people and of themselves can become more and more problematic as they move through their lives.

Life and Love at Arm's Length

My coaching client Giselle has struggled with the pain of distrust all her life. In our initial coaching session, she described the pain point of distrust as a 10 on a scale of 1 to 10. "I crave being closer to people, but the thought of closeness and connection petrifies me. I throw up all sorts of walls and boundaries. I sabotage my relationships. Honestly, I think all my relationships are based on control — me trying to control everything — and so it feels like no relationship I have is ever real."

You can hear in Giselle's words the beliefs she stores in her mind about her ability to trust. Her thoughts center on her need to control her relationships to keep her safe from rejection and loss. The experiences she's gathered, in relation to broken trust, stand as her proof that authentic and real connections are not possible for her, so she avoids and even sabotages opportunities for closeness.

Many adoptees have shared with me their feelings of holding people at arm's length because they believe they can't trust letting them in. They often speak of drawing lines in the sand as a way to protect themselves. They share their feelings of how trusting themselves and their own decisions seems impossible. Some say that they sit around daily and wait for the next bad thing — the next abandonment or letdown — to happen. So they isolate and disconnect. My client Debra shared with me, "Perhaps the only thing I trust is the belief that it's all going to unravel and go away, so why invest my emotions in something or someone that's sure to disappear?"

While trust is an essential part of life, it's also a fragile part of life, whether or not you are adopted. Trust asks of us to have faith in people and in situations without any guarantees of the outcome. In all our flawed humanness, trust will be, at some point, damaged when one person lets another down. The destruction of trust caused by a first parent leaving is severe. For the adoptee, it can also be a predictor of future untrustworthiness.

So many of an adoptee's reactions to distrust are unconscious, which can make life and love very challenging. I have spent years on unconscious high alert, just waiting for someone I love to leave. I have sacrificed my own values as I distrusted my own voice and made relationship decisions that were not healthy or right for me. At times I even played a dangerous game of trusting in people I knew were truly untrustworthy because when they let me down, it reinforced my belief that trusting was a no-win situation. These behavior patterns were unconscious but a dynamic I needed to address in order to build a bridge back to trust, both of myself and of others.

Teresa and the Traps of Distrust

Teresa first came to me when her struggle with distrust became, in her words, "destructive and out of hand." She shared in our first session that she had been having one-night encounters, as she characterized them, because in her words, "I know that it will be over in the morning. I don't have to wait around in agonizing uncertainty." For Teresa this behavior pattern felt safer than committing to a relationship that she believed would abruptly end at some point. She went on to add, "I feel such a sense of guilt and shame when I wake up from a casual encounter. The guilt and shame I feel are glaring reminders that I can't even trust my own decisions."

Teresa's behavior patterns were damaging to her sense of

self-worth. She was choosing one-night encounters to fill her time and to feel in control. Yet these brief moments only left her feeling empty and ashamed. In addition, these encounters served to strengthen her belief that she couldn't trust her own decisions. She "bolted" when a connection felt like it could be real. For Teresa, connections that might be meaningful seemed too good to be true. She didn't view herself as worthy of something deep and lasting. "All the guilt and shame just keep stacking up in my head." Teresa was trapped in a place of debilitating distrust. I worked with her to help bring her to a conscious recognition of these unconscious behavior patterns that were hurting her and, ultimately, keeping her from forging a foundation of healthy trust in her life.

—⚡︎—

ADOPTEE AWAKENING: *Adoptees can start to consciously recognize the trust turbulence in their lives and to take action to calm and diminish this chaos.*

In a moment I'm going to share with you the steps that I guided both Teresa and Giselle through to help them build a healthy foundation of trust. These are tools I use for myself and many of the adoptees who come to me struggling with the pain of distrust. First, though, I'd like to move through some of the ways adoptees may test the waters of trust in relationships. I call these unconscious patterns of behavior "push-pull." It's vital that adoptees and those who care about them become aware of these potential patterns and seek adoptee-informed support when needed.

The Push-Pull Pattern

Just a few months ago, I coached a woman who was in a romantic relationship with an adoptee. She felt her partner pulling away from her and couldn't understand why, and she felt rejected and hurt. I explained to her that while she feels rejection in her relationship, her partner *fears* rejection and this could be why he falls into the pattern of pulling away and pushing her away. He could be harboring unconscious distrust fueled by his unresolved fear of rejection and abandonment.

This woman had read an article on my website on the push-pull pattern. In it I wrote that, as an adoptee, I've done a good amount of pushing and pulling in my own life. I've pushed people away for fear that they might leave me first. And I've pulled away as a test to see if they'd come back. I've pushed the door closed on relationships because I didn't trust they would last. I've pulled my feelings down deep within me in hopes that the hurt would disappear. It didn't. I've pushed and hustled to prove my worth, yet I still felt uncertain of my value. I didn't trust that I held any value at all.

I've pushed and hustled to be viewed as perfect by others because I believed that imperfect things — imperfect people — would be sent back. I was terrified that my imperfections would lead to further rejection; I didn't trust that they might have something to teach me. I didn't trust that the imperfect parts of me could have value. I didn't understand that perfection doesn't exist. I would pull away from others because I saw them as perfect and myself as broken and flawed. I didn't trust that I had anything to offer. I didn't know that the quest for perfection, an impossible goal, only leaves a person feeling more and more disappointed in and distrusting of themselves.

I've pushed to go back and relive the parts of my life that disappeared without my consent. I've pushed to make people proud of me — sometimes people I didn't even know. Yet, I didn't trust that I could ever be proud of myself. I've pushed and I've pulled to run from the shame and the guilt that I felt inside. There are so many ways that adoptees can unconsciously fall into this pattern of push-pull.

So often I hear the loved ones of adoptees say, "They keep push-ing me away." I want you to understand that the pushing is not aimed to hurt you — it's not personal. It's an unconscious act of self-protection for the adoptee. It's a survival technique that kicks in quickly and often without notice because a part of the adoptee feels so exposed and at risk. They want to stay in control and ahead of the pain because distrust has a cruel grip on their life. Yet these push-pull behaviors lead to long-term suffering for adoptees.

For a person in a relationship with an adoptee, whether that be a romantic relationship, a friendship, or a parent-child relationship, the push-pull pattern can look like the following:

1. You may feel as if you are constantly being tested. Do you really mean what you say? Do you really want to be with the adoptee? Do you really love the adoptee? Your love may be put to the test. The adoptee may try to make you prove that you love them or struggle with how you could possibly love them when they struggle to even love themselves.

2. If you pass the test, it may be only temporary because the adoptee may still be struggling with feelings of in-security and distrust.

3. The adoptee may not allow you to get too close to them — or may at times feel agitated when you reach out to touch them — which can represent a core lack of trust.

4. The adoptee may not want you to get too far away from them because it's triggering for them. An adoptee may view your distance as a potential threat. They may even wonder if you've found another person to take their place. This all comes from a sense of shame and unworthiness.

5. It may be difficult for the adoptee to believe that you love them. Perhaps they are constantly wanting you to

prove your love to them, which can represent a core lack of self-love, self-esteem, and self-concept.

6. The adoptee may have continual thoughts you are looking for something or someone better.

The pain of distrust is found in all the ways that we, as adoptees, push others away and pull ourselves away. As a former foster child and adoptee, I understand just how hard it is to trust. I understand the pain of hearing that voice inside your head asking, "Will they leave, too?"

I know how frightening it is when you believe that the voice of distrust will never go away. I know how fragile you can feel when life is lived on a thin piece of ice. At any moment, the ice can crack and everything can disappear. I know how disempowering it is when you believe that you're not even worthy of your own trust. It can feel so lonely. Yet I go back to my strong belief that trust starts with a promise to never abandon yourself. Distrust of self is the ultimate betrayal. Building that muscle of self-trust is essential and is step 1 along the journey of regaining a sense of lasting trust.

I was driving my teenage son home from high school football practice recently when I asked him his views on trust. He was adopted from Russia when he was eleven months old, so I was very interested in getting his take on the topic as we've journeyed to build a bridge back to trust as mother and son. "I think that trust starts from the inside, Mom. It's an inside-out sort of thing. You taught me that! I like to show up for myself every day. Doing this builds a sense of self-confidence, and that builds a solid foundation of self-trust. You've got to trust yourself first." I followed his comment with a saying I hadn't heard in a very long time: "If you can't trust yourself, who can you trust?"

These insightful comments were spoken by a young man who was once a little boy afraid of being touched because he was petrified to trust. I spent so many nights holding him and reassuring him with my words and presence. I'd say, "Son, I'm never leaving and I pray that my loving actions will be the proof you need to trust me. I also pray that you will grow to love and trust yourself." As I drove with my son on the way home from practice that day, I realized that's just who he had become — a young man of international adoption who loves and trusts himself. A son who feels safe to trust in the bond we have created over time.

There is no question that abandonment can shift the adoptee's foundational knowing of trust. The really good news is that we can become more aware of the push-pull patterns and work to lessen their negative impact. We can do this through a deeper understanding of what intuition is and how we can reclaim our connection with our intuitive nature.

Giselle and Teresa are adult adopted women who came to me suffering from the turbulence that distrust was causing in their lives. You'll recall that Giselle craved closeness and connection but was petrified of both. She found herself sabotaging relationships due to her high level of distrust. Teresa's intense amount of distrust had caused "destructive and out-of-hand" behavior patterns that resulted in her carrying around a great deal of guilt and shame. In fact, both these women carried guilt and shame to varying degrees.

The self-awareness that came from the following exercises, and continues to come, has helped to decrease the intensity of this pain point for them both. This increased awareness has also helped to calm the stormy waters of distrust, along with the associated feelings of shame and guilt. Teresa's pain point level has moved from a 10 to a 5.5, and Giselle's has moved from an 8.5 to a 4, in a relatively short amount of time.

Before we move forward with the exercises, I do want to stress that not all adoptees struggle with the pain of distrust. Every adoptee story is as individual as the adopted person. Adoptees may experience some of the pain points in this book, all of them, or none of them. And that's completely okay.

It's very important that we hold space for all adoptee experiences and to provide resources that meet them where they are along their journey. And the journey will evolve. A pain point that's never shown up before may show up as an adoptee moves through the seasons of their life. That's completely okay, too. The goal is to make sure that adoptees can always find a supportive place to be compassionately witnessed — be it within the pages of a book, in a support group, in therapy or life coaching, or inside a safe relationship.

—⁓—

ADOPTEE AWAKENING: *Trust starts with a promise to never abandon yourself.*

REFLECTION EXERCISE
Creating a Healthy Landscape of Self-Trust

Take a deep breath in and a long exhale out. You're moving through these pages and exercises and giving yourself the gift of awakening to inner places that have been waiting for you. How does knowing that feel? You're moving forward and doing the brave work of self-discovery – acknowledge yourself for that!

Now I'd like you to grab your journal and reflect on the following question: *What do I need from myself in order to trust myself more?* Take that in for a moment. Read this question a few more times if needed. This is a question of self-awareness. Do you feel like trust in yourself has been fractured? How and in what ways have those fractures occurred? I'd like you to explore what you believe you need, from yourself, in order to begin healing those fractured places and creating a healthy and sustainable landscape of self-trust in your life.

It may be that you need more stillness in your day so that

you can connect to the voice within. You may need to practice repeating affirmations to yourself that support you and keep you motivated and in alignment with your values. Perhaps you need to offer yourself a kind dose of forgiveness and grace. Or maybe you need to focus on building that muscle of self-credibility as you commit to showing up for yourself, each and every day — mind, body, and spirit. What would that look like for you? Whatever it is, please take time to reflect and journal on this question: *What do I need from myself in order to trust myself more?*

I've found this question to be such a beautiful offering to myself as I wait for answers and awaken ways that support and increase my levels of self-trust. This reflection exercise is a great way to forge a beautiful inner dialogue with yourself. Take a few moments and continue to reflect and go within. When you are ready, we'll move on to our reframing exercise.

I'd like to add that this question of reflection can also be reworded and redirected to the adoptee you care about. It's a healing way to enter into caring conversation when you find yourself in a push-pull pattern. You can ask the adoptee, in a safe space where you are focused and making eye contact, open and heartfully engaged: What do you need from me in order for you to trust me more? As a parent, I find this to be an excellent question to ask my kids. It's brought about some incredibly profound moments of truth and healing.

This question works as long as each person is willing to hear the other and give of themselves in a vulnerable and loving way. What I offer in this chapter and in this book are alternative approaches that I have learned through my coaching experiences and in my own experiences as an adoptee, woman, and mother. I offer up the tools and approaches that I know have worked for me and so many others. It's an honor to share them with you.

The Wisdom of Intuition

Now that you've journaled on what you need from yourself in order to build a strong foundation of self-trust, I'd like to talk about intuition. I define *intuition* as knowledge that doesn't reside in the brain. It's a deep and innate knowing that's outside the traditional intellect. Basically, intuition means that we know something without having to think about it. If you're not really familiar with intuition, that's okay; there was a time when I wasn't either. For many years, I wasn't connected to my intuitive compass or tuned in to an internal guidance system. As adoptees, we can tune back in to these places within ourselves. That's the really encouraging news!

During that time of disconnection in my life, there was a lot of loud chatter in my head. Maybe you can relate. The noise in my mind kept me tuned out from a softer voice that wanted to speak to me. That softer voice was my own intuition. If I closed my eyes, I could vaguely remember a time as a young girl when I felt connected with that intuitive place of wisdom. Over the years, though, that connection became more and more fractured. I lost faith in my intuition, and distrust quickly moved in. I didn't know how to cultivate a relationship with myself and grow in self-trust.

It wasn't until I began sitting in stillness and practicing meditation that I could hear the whispers of my heart and the soft and subtle voice of intuition. Building a relationship with my intuitive places has helped me, over time, to regain self-trust and to awaken spiritually to my divine ability to trust in my voice and in my decisions. That required me to slow down and to listen to what my body — my internal and emotional ecosystem — was telling me. I can't say that sitting with myself in stillness was easy at first. It was actually a little scary because I'd never allowed myself the space to be still and receive my internal wisdom.

Yet taking that deep dive within and immersing myself in a calm that I'd never felt before offered me a window into what trust

in myself, in my voice, and in my intuition looked like. These discoveries required that I make space for my heart to speak, my gut
wisdom to rise, and my feelings to be honored and experienced. In
these moments of deep and immersive calm, I began to note the
difference between the logical mind, the heart intuition, and the
gut intuition.

You know the saying "Just go with your gut?" There's a good
reason for that saying. The gut is actually known as the second
brain. It's lined with a network of 100 million nerve cells, fewer
than the brain's 86 billion neurons, true, but I use these numbers to
show that there's a whole lot going on in your gut. Your gut actually
communicates with your brain!

Often we're conditioned to listen just to the mind. We can get
caught up in irrational thoughts, overanalyzing and overthinking
when we do. When that happens, we can forget that a wealth of
knowledge and divine perspective resides in our hearts and our guts.

So many things can trigger adoptees to override their intuition
and land in a place of deep distrust. Sometimes it's not just one
thing; it can be many things that leave adoptees feeling void of an
ability to trust. For me, relinquishment by my first mother, abandonment by my first father, and life in an adoptive home where
one parent was addicted to alcohol provided a feeding ground for
distrust to grow. The evidence strengthened my belief that parents
couldn't be trusted. No one could really be trusted. First parents
leave. Adoptive parents can, too. Countries and cultures of origin
can be removed. Self-identity, self-worth, and self-confidence can
be erased.

Adoptees can become stuck in the mind and mute the subtle
sounds of their heart and gut wisdom. Often that leads to feelings
of dread, anxiety, or the need to multitask to the point where they
don't connect with the present moment. If you find yourself using
phrases like "I'm trying to figure it out" or "I'm working on making

a decision," you are likely in the mind. In those moments of battling with uncertainty and distrust, try holding open the choice you have to make or the question that you are in need of answering. Hold it open to your heart intuition and your gut intuition. Listen and watch for what your intuition has to say.

As adoptees, we need to get curious about what our heart and gut intuition want to communicate to us. What if you dropped down into your beautiful heart space and listened for the wisdom it holds? What if you breathed deeply and dropped down into your courageous gut space and listened for the words it wants to share? What if you could open up a portal of communication to listen, acknowledge, trust, and believe in your intuition? How might that transform your belief in trusting yourself, your voice, and your ability to make decisions that are healthy, whole, and right for you? What if, from this day forward, you never forgot that your body holds a wealth of intuitive knowledge that is there to guide you forward to a life that is flourishing and authentic?

REFRAMING EXERCISE
Inviting In Intuition

Making contact with your intuition is a beautiful gift to give yourself. Here's the thing: not even removal, relinquishment, or adoption can take our intuition from us. We may lose contact with it for a time, but adoptees are capable of reconnecting those lines of intuitive communication. I want to help you do that, now, through this adoptee self-trust meditation.

Adoptee Self-Trust Meditation

- Get comfortable in a seated position of your choice. Let your arms fall naturally in your lap, with palms facing up.

- When you are settled in and ready, please close your eyes.
- Take three deep breaths in through your nose, and exhale fully through your mouth. On the exhale, release any tension you may be feeling in your body.
- After your third deep inhale and complete exhale, go back to breathing normally through your nose. Continue to notice any tension in your body, and gently release that tension as you breathe.
- Now I want to invite you to travel deep inside yourself. I'd like you to visualize your first me – the beautiful child within you with whom you have done the integrity-filled work of reconnecting. Continue to breathe as you see that child sitting in a light-filled place within you.
- This child that you see, your first me, trusts their intuition, doesn't second-guess their thoughts, and isn't afraid of learning from their mistakes.
- There was a time when the current version of you stopped having faith in your abilities. This version of you, along your adoptee journey, dimmed its light and became small in order to stay safe.
- You stopped trusting in what you saw and felt. You stopped trusting in your intuition. You stopped believing in your ability to trust. Forgive yourself for all that.
- Now imagine your first me – still sitting in that beautiful wash of light – ready to reconnect to your greatness. Ready to plug back in to the innate intuition of you.
- Feel that sensation. Be with it for as long as you like. Notice your feelings.
- Your first me, that earliest version of you, is ready to

disconnect from the limiting story that told you to stop trusting.

- Allow that early version of you to start expanding. Let the light surrounding your first me expand, too, and let them both fill your very being to overflow.
- Once they've reached this place of overflow, you have allowed your trusting self to step into the forefront. You feel a confidence and a clarity taking over. You feel an increased ability to make choices that align with your truest values, needs, and desires.
- Now repeat after me: I listen to my intuition — my beautiful inner wisdom. I recognize my unique abilities. I believe in the power of my lived experiences as an adoptee. I will use my intuition, my unique abilities, and my lived experiences to inform and direct me without doubting or second-guessing myself.
- Hold this version of you that has emerged — this version that has always lived within you — and let it take up space in the foreground. Let it step forward, out of the shadows and out of the fog. How does that feel? Be with the feeling for as long as you desire.
- Take a deep breath in, and then let out a long exhale.
- When you are ready, open your eyes.

Use this meditation whenever you need it. It's here to support you in this walk of intuitive trusting, living, and loving. My coaching clients Giselle and Teresa use this meditation often. Anytime they find themselves falling into an old pattern of distrust, they go to it. Anytime they feel uncertain about a decision that's in front of them, they turn to it. It has changed how they view their ability to trust themselves and ultimately their ability to trust others.

Now that you've been guided through this self-trust meditation, journal on the question that you were asked earlier: *What do I need from myself in order to trust myself more?* See if anything new comes up for you. Do you need to set healthier boundaries, make an oath to be a promise keeper to yourself, commit to self-care, or be more aware of your emotions and the words you use with yourself? These commitments kept — no matter how big or small — will lead to massive transformation in the area of self-trust. That in exchange will lead to more authentic connections in every aspect of your life.

In the next chapter, we'll explore pain point number 6, the pain of banished biology. The pain of banished biology can be challenging for those who feel they need to hide what is real, who feel they need to be someone else in order to be accepted and loved. Together we'll identify what aspects of your biology may feel most exiled from you. We'll take steps to free that part of you from a place of banishment, identify ways to experience your truest nature, and discover points of grace along the way.

Adoptee Affirmation

I am worthy of my trust.
I am capable of trusting.
I am deserving of a life complete with trust-filled connections.

Chapter Seven

Longing for Reflections

The Pain of Banished Biology

Adoptees know that biology matters. We understand that knowing at least a part of our original story anchors us, yet for a very long time we've been at sea, tossed around by a different narrative. As adopted people, we feel our biology pulsing within us, even if we don't believe we are safe to openly express it.

Adoptees often feel that others see their biology as irrelevant. Mentally, emotionally, and physically, the exiling of our origins has taken a heavy toll. It's like being stranded out in the ocean and between two shores. You want to swim toward the shore of biology to explore, but you're no longer sure if you have permission to go there.

Many adoptees feel this exiling from a very young age, especially if there has been no safe container for them to explore and express their original story. As we know, it's simply not true that gaining an adoptive family completely erases the memories and wonderings about the adoptee's past. It just doesn't work that way.

Before my adoptive family moved to America with me, we made memories trekking through Europe in a refurbished VW van. Even as a little girl, I remember searching for a sense of belonging as we wandered through southern Europe. A favorite image from that time is of me running and playing near the Leaning Tower of Pisa, in Italy. It remains one of my happiest childhood recollections.

People in southern Europe thought that I was "one of them," regardless of what country we were in. In Italy the locals would come up to my family and say, "Bella, bella, she must be Italian!" For a child who looked nothing like her adoptive family, being claimed by strangers in this way — with such heartfelt enthusiasm — offered a comforting feeling of belonging, even if the feeling lasted only a few short moments. I recall having my antennas up as I continually scanned the crowds in those European villages, trying to find somewhere that felt familiar or someone who looked familiar. In my adoptive family, I had no mirroring of my physical appearance. My olive-toned skin, dark-brown eyes, and black hair were so different from that of my adoptive family, whose features were much lighter than mine. No one around me knew that I had such strong internal questions about who I was and who I belonged to.

I was known to wander away and disappear in those European campgrounds. I didn't ask permission to go, and I didn't announce my leaving. My mother would be preparing the evening's meal and would casually look up to find me gone. My parents never had any great sense of panic. They were sure that I was close and out on one of my grand solo adventures.

Mom would send my adoptive older brothers out on a mission of search and retrieval. "Please, go find your sister," she'd tell them. My brothers would go around calling out my name and asking nearby campers if they'd seen a little girl, with black hair and big brown eyes, wandering the campsites alone. Eventually, I'd be found sitting on the ground, happily eating with strangers.

My family believed it was my appetite for corn that would cause me to wander off into foreign camping areas. That may have been the case in part because I always did adore a buttery corn on the cob. What my family didn't know was that I possessed an even greater appetite for belonging. In every campsite I stumbled on, I was hungry to see myself in the face of someone else. I didn't know who I was. My true identity was a mystery to me. I was longing for reflections of my own biology.

Many adoptees who come to me for coaching are in a place of longing, too. They long to crack the code of their biology and reconnect to that inherited and essential part of who they are. It's a courageous journey of clearing the fog of assigned identity, assigned nationality, and assigned culture that happens through adoption. No doubt this clearing journey can be especially poignant for adoptees of international adoption and/or transracial adoption in which a child is adopted into a family of a race or ethnicity that is different from their own. Yet even children who have been adopted within their own culture, country or ethnicity long for this kind of clearing. They may be offered more reflections of their own background but still have a lingering hunger to know more of their truest nature.

There is a saying in Spanish, "*La sangre es fuerte*," meaning "blood is strong." We can never forget that adoptees, no matter their adoption arrangement, will likely feel the pulse of their origins within them and may long to know more. It's incredibly difficult when, as an adoptee, you're told who you are by the outside world yet feel like a very different person on the inside. It's excruciating when you don't believe you can open the door to those places inside yourself that were there before your adoption ever happened. It's like trying to grasp hold of someone who is just beyond your reach.

As we discussed in chapter 4, an immense amount of personal information and biological family history is often locked away and unavailable to adoptees. If the information is available, it often takes nearly an act of Congress for an adoptee to gain access to it. For international/transnational adoptees, a personal history of the bio family can be virtually nonexistent. The case is the same for medical history. Depending on where an adoptee is born, their earliest information — whether or not completely factual, as in the assigning of a birthday because the actual birth date is not known, may be contained in a thick file or a paper-thin one.

Some adoptees may not fully know their original ancestry. They may walk around feeling a sense of connection to certain music or certain foods, certain places or certain smells, and not understand why. They may scan a busy crowd of strangers and ask themselves, *Could that be my mother? Could that man be my father?* Adoptees may travel somewhere and feel like they've been there before, as if a certain part of themselves holds a link to the past that they are not aware of. I always urge my coaching clients to take note when those sensations hit them. I believe each and every time it's a clue.

I first met my bio half brother, Antonio, in Spain, after discovering him while searching for our father, Juliáno. The first time I phoned Antonio, his line rang eight times before he answered. "Hello Antonio, this is Michelle. I'm your sister in America." My brother replied, "Yes, I know." We cried for a few moments over the passing of our father and the many years spent apart. We then dedicated ourselves to a plan of meeting each other and began to talk of many things. Much of our phone conversation, of course, was about the father we shared. I was grateful to Antonio for letting me peek through the curtain of what life was like for him while growing up with my first father, his only father. I was thirsty to soak in as much information as possible! Once Antonio and I had the opportunity to meet, many more truths came to light.

Two surprising and validating insights came from our time together during our reunion in Spain. The first was that both Antonio and I had an insatiable craving for Spanish olives. As kids we would both eat entire jars of olives and then drink the juice. It may seem like a small similarity, but for me, it was huge. I'd never had that kind of quirky connection with a sibling before.

The second truth that came from my reunion with Antonio

was that, like me, my first father loved dandelions. When I was a little girl, I would sit for hours in an open field near my home in America. The field sat at the end of a long, dusty road. I'd run there alone on some afternoons in eager anticipation of what awaited me. My white sneakers would be covered in dirt by the time I arrived. I knew my mother wouldn't be pleased, but I didn't care. It felt rebellious. I liked that feeling. Taking a deep breath, I'd yelp with glee as I plunged into the tall grasses and disappeared. My eyes would immediately begin scanning the ground for dandelions. They were why I had come.

I recall how the sun felt warm on my cheeks as I held my face up to the sky and let my hands explore the earth for hidden treasures. My smile grew from ear to ear when my fingers would touch the tiny white puffs of magic. "There you are," I'd whisper. One by one, I'd gently pluck the dandelions from the soil, placing them close to my lips. Practice had proven that short, quick puffs of air gave the seeds the lift they needed. For some reason, I'd think of my first father as I watched, with pure delight, those dandelions being carried off on the breeze. He always came to my mind during these moments of dandelion escape, and I'd fantasize about what he might be like and how he might even love me. I'd imagine him flying through the sky, like those precious dandelion seeds — floating high above earth looking for a way to find me, his *hija*.

During our reunion in Spain, Antonio confirmed to me that our father had been a paratrooper. This was something that had been suggested to me by my first mother while visiting her in England as a teenager — information also confirmed in the foster records I received later in life. During our reunion, Antonio also shared that our father, in Spain, loved to blow on dandelions. He'd blow on them while standing on a bridge overlooking a creek and guess where the little puffs might land.

When I learned of that story, the dandelion became even more significant to me. It was important to my first father and I believe connected us over the miles, crossing borders — those banished places — that neither of us could cross. These borders kept us physically separated, yet somehow the dandelion united us in the sky and in spirit. I could feel this connection as a girl. I hold hope that Juliáno felt this connection, too.

I've read that the dandelion signifies healing from emotional pain, a spiritual intelligence, and a personal warmth not commonly found. Perhaps this is true. I can only express the sensation I had as a girl of feeling connected to my first father when I'd blow on dandelions. I didn't have to apologize for that connection. I didn't have to hide it or explain it away. I only had to feel it. And the warm feeling that surged through my young being was healing and, yes, it was spiritual.

The dandelion has become my eternal connection to my first father. To this day, when I pluck a dandelion from the earth and hold it in my hands, I feel held by my father. It feels like I'm holding him, too. I say a prayer and blow that same puff of air that I blew as a rebellious little girl. I watch as the dandelion explodes like fireworks into the sky. It's on the breeze where my father and I find each other. It's where we've always found each other.

The olives and dandelions are two of the clues to my biological story that I have come across in this journey as an adoptee. It's been my experience that staying curious is key. Noticing the feelings, sensations, and signs that may cross the adoptee's path is one essential way of allowing parts of their biology to speak to them and connect them to places within that feel left behind.

Becoming Super Observers as Adoptees

Notice what you notice! I say this all the time to the amazing adoptees I have the privilege of coaching. I cannot overstress just how vital it is that adoptees be allowed to keep open these pathways of discovery along their journey of reconnection and reclamation. Every adoptee should be encouraged and supported in being a super observer of the feelings, sensations, and signs that make them tingle or come alive inside. These things are clues, little pebbles creating ripple effects that lead the adoptee closer to home within as they begin to awaken their biology.

As for me, I've dived deep into my own journey of biological discovery. I've free-fallen into places I never imagined I would ever go. I've even been a risk-taker in an effort to more deeply connect to the sensations that connect me to my first father. I was longing, since the youngest of age, to feel those connections to him.

During my childhood years, I had felt an inner sensation of my first father in flight, floating over me and watching over me. During one of my visits to England as a teen, my first mother told me of my father's passionate love of skydiving. When I grew into adulthood, my curiosity about my father's passion didn't leave me. While working as a television news anchor and correspondent, I had the opportunity to train for a skydiving maneuver with the Golden Knights, the elite aerial parachute demonstration team for the US Army.

I remember free-falling from the plane at some eleven thousand feet, over Yuma, Arizona, and experiencing the exhilaration of the moment. I was flying at a speed of 135 miles an hour, and there was nothing I could do but surrender to the moment. As an adoptee who had searched for some sense of certainty through trying to control things, this surrendering was a life lesson — an experiment in uncertainty — that I needed to experience. As the parachute opened and I began to float peacefully toward the earth, I thought of the freedom that my father must have felt as a paratrooper, through both the free fall and the floating. I became a super observer of the sensations going on within me and around me.

The message that came to me while I was floating toward my landing spot was that my first father loved to be in flight. He loved the complete surrender of the moment. As I experienced skydiving for myself on that day, I realized that I loved the feeling of complete surrender as well. It wasn't as scary as I had thought it would be. Surrender meant letting go and letting in new beliefs about how to truly live. I didn't need to fight so hard. This awakening came to me as I floated peacefully — nothing but me, the gentle rush of air, the beauty of the sky, the land below, and thoughts of my father.

The experience of skydiving was a moment of spiritual connection to my first father that stays with me to this day. Juliáno liked the feeling of freedom in flight. He'd passed that on to me. I think that's why today I love flying over rails on my horse. I feel connected to something bigger than myself. And, as I sit here writing these words to you, I can feel the rush as I went free-falling from that plane over Arizona. I can feel my body quickly reorganizing itself and learning how to breathe during the free fall. I can feel the peace of floating beneath the canopy of a parachute that opened up and was carrying me home. I can feel the spiritual connection to my father. I remember feeling a little less banished. It was a beautiful moment of flight, faith, and forgiveness.

Skydiving with the Golden Knights taught me that if I can free-fall from a plane at eleven thousand feet, then I can do anything. I revisit that sensation often whenever I forget the vastness of who I am. I truly believe that my first father was parenting me during that skydiving experience. He led me to that place, and I'm so glad I followed. I'm so glad I allowed myself to surrender.

Ultimately, my first father didn't need to physically be there with me in Yuma. I just needed to allow him in — spiritually. I urge all adoptees to go beyond their preconceived limits to discover more of who they are and to free-fall — deeper and deeper — into those places within that hold answers of peace, surrender, and otherworldly connection to their origins. A wealth of information can be found in those sacred places inside.

—⚏—

ADOPTEE AWAKENING: *Adoptees can become super ob-servers of the signs that are waiting to bring them closer and closer to their origins.*

DNA Testing

It would be impossible to talk about the exploration of biology with-out speaking about DNA testing because it's transformed the way adoptees are discovering their ethnicity, biological connections to potential birth family members, medical information, and unique family origins. Many adoptees, depending on the structure of their adoption and the legal framework around it, see DNA tests as their last, or only, resort when for decades they've been blocked from accessing pertinent information about their identity and biology.

This is beginning to change with the wider embrace of open adoption, yet there remains a large community of adoptees who still live with archaic laws that continue to discriminate against and mar-ginalize their community. They can feel discouraged as they spend years battling the many roadblocks in their search for facts. With a long history of sealed documents and closed adoptions, many adop-tees hold little legal right to their own biological information. The basic human right of access to this information needs to be recog-nized and given back to adoptees. Day in and day out, however, adoptees hear very few voices in the halls of power speaking on their behalf. DNA testing has become a necessary step for adoptees along the all-too-often complicated quest to discover their roots.

Indeed, the journey of discovery through DNA testing can offer transformative insights for adoptees. It certainly has for me, and I've witnessed this transformation in the lives of the adoptees I coach. If you go this route, however, it's vital that you be pre-pared for how quickly you may be linked to close biological family members — even if your initial intent in testing was simply to find out more about your genetics and ethnicity. It's also important to be prepared for a slower discovery process if you're from a place in the world where DNA testing may not be as accessible.

If an adoptee is linked to their bio family, it's also crucial to note that even the best of adoption reunions — if DNA testing leads to that moment — can have bumps, unexpected curves, and detours in the road. It's essential that the adoptee be prepared to step into a reunion and has an understanding that, no matter the outcome, they are whole and complete within themselves. It's hard if not impossible to shut the door once it's been opened through a DNA test, so be aware of the potential pitfalls as well as the potential benefits.

I strongly encourage you to organize a solid support network before doing a DNA test because you never know what you might find or what your reactions to those findings may be. I often coach adoptees before, during, and after the DNA testing process. Whether you access the support of a life coach, therapist, other adoptees, or reliable family members and friends, designating a safe space to turn to for reflection and guidance is key because taking a test can be a challenging and sometimes traumatizing experience. You may discover things you didn't really want to know. If so, ask yourself a variation of the question on page 107: *How can I see this as happening* for *me and not* to *me?* This question is like a guiding star that can help you keep on course and not be derailed by DNA information that may be difficult to process.

Do your own research before embarking on the DNA journey, and listen to the experiences of other adoptees who have done the test. Most important, be gentle with yourself. So much of our lives as adoptees has been dictated by others. The journey back to ourselves should be carried out in a way that best aligns with our needs.

It's also important to state that DNA testing may not — and

likely won't — fill in all the missing pieces of the adoptee's story. I cannot stress enough that the decision of whether or not to take a DNA test should always be completely up to the adoptee. They should never feel cornered or coerced to take a test. It is not for everyone, and that's okay. DNA testing as well as genealogical research is about the adoptee's individual needs, wants, and comfort levels. Any and all research and testing should be carried out in the adoptee's own time, at their own pace, and in their own way.

Micaela and Hailey Discover Their Biological Identities

My coaching client Micaela told me, "I kept my expectations low as I moved through the DNA testing. I knew that if I found a match, I still might not be provided with all the answers I'm looking for. I did find my bio father, though, and that has been really important for me. He's ill and so my time with him is limited. It's been both bitter and sweet. I have a strong support network, and they have helped me to feel seen and heard."

Another client, Hailey, came to me with a desire to know the truth of her ethnicity. She'd been told all her life that she was of biracial background: Caucasian and Polynesian. For some reason, that assigned description never felt right to her. "I want to take a DNA test so that I can know for sure my true ethnicity." Hailey described her level of pain at a 9.5 on a scale of 10, as she struggled with the hurt of a banished biology.

I worked with Hailey to prepare her for whatever DNA results came back. During the process, I asked her to enter a place of meditation and stillness to ask the question, *What is my true racial identity?* When Hailey did, the voice that answered said that she was indeed biracial — but Caucasian and Black. Hailey had always felt that she was Black, but her adoptive mother stressed otherwise and in any conversation would close the door on the topic. The DNA test results proved what Hailey had always known to be true inside.

Her bio mother was white and her bio father Black. "It's such a relief to confirm what I've always felt to be true," she said.

As adoptees, I believe we hold an innate knowing of ourselves, yet we're programmed to forget these places inside us. Whether or not this programming is intentional, we're taught that we must become someone else in order to be loved and accepted, cared for and embraced. When we enter a place of meditation and stillness, we can ask for any blocks to be removed, for any lingering story that shuts down our truest nature to be cleared. Inside this inspiration, I've experienced my own intuition leading me toward an inner truth of my biology and I've also witnessed clients — like Hailey — emerge into their own sense of authentic identity and the remembering of who they are beyond what they've been told.

Not everyone in Hailey's adoptive family accepted the truth that came from her personal work and that was supported by her DNA test results. Her mother was not willing to accept the test results. She took it as an offense that Hailey even felt the need to take the test. As hard and disappointing as this was for Hailey, she empowered herself through setting healthy boundaries and seeking support from other adoptees.

Hailey moved forward with a possible reunion with her paternal bio family. As she did, she allowed herself to feel the grief of a banished biology. We spent many sessions in a gentle container of understanding as Hailey released the grief that she'd felt forced to bottle up for so many years. She let her emotions flow. It was a much-needed cleansing that allowed for a great deal of healing.

The grief that adoptees feel over their banished biology is yet another place of loss that adoptees are so often required to hide. In our sessions, Hailey began to give voice to those places. She said, "The Black side of me has always been pushed within the shadows. I'm finally shining a light on that part of who I am, and it feels really good."

Hailey also prepared for a reunion through emails with her paternal bio family members and through scheduling phone calls with her bio father. She took her time with this process and nurtured these new connections over several months. Hailey also prepared for the moment of reunion by regulating her nervous system through breath work and continued meditation, along with the consistent journaling of her thoughts, questions, and feelings as she allowed herself to express what was coming up for her.

Hailey organized a safe support system with trusted friends and fellow adoptees and was transparent about her needs. She also created picture books of her life to share with her bio family once she reunited with them. In addition, Hailey created a vision board to help her visualize herself within a reunion. She said, "As I take all these steps, I feel more empowered. I don't want to continue living a lie about who I am. I feel ready to take this trip of reunion, with no expectations, and to learn more of my history."

Reunion with her paternal bio family was emotional, exhilarating, and draining for Hailey. She described the experience as "almost being in a state of shock but not in a negative way." Her paternal bio family was and continues to be supportive and embracing of her. Most of all, however, Hailey has grown more supportive and embracing of herself through this process of claiming her racial identity and reuniting with her paternal bio family. She's really come into her own and has reduced her pain from a 9.5 to a 2 on the scale.

As Hailey's coach, it's been truly remarkable to witness her journey of transformation. She said, "I felt like I was the one with the holes, and my bio family members helped to fill them. Maybe I've helped them to fill some holes, too. One thing is for sure, I don't feel so alone anymore! Now I can openly share this part of who I am with my children because this is a part of who they are, too. I can share with them this energy of knowing our roots — our Black roots! I can continue to grow this energy and move forward with the things I want to do in my life. I didn't have that sense of knowing before. Now I do. I'm not going to let anyone take that from me again. I'm not bitter, but I sure am getting better!"

I want to stress that every adoptee reunion is unique and will hold its own set of dynamics, time frames, and discoveries. It's highly advised that adoptees do not enter this journey with hard-and-fast expectations but with a sense of appreciation for how they're showing up for themselves and taking ownership of their biology and identity. Beyond DNA testing, adoptees can seek additional support through vetted search angels. These are individuals and groups that can assist with online technical support and offer their genetic genealogical expertise to adoptees searching for biological information. Most important, adoptees should do their research and ask lots of questions. Remember, this is your search — when and if you're ready — so connect with your power and make it your own!

My adoptive mother used to tell me that I was "white and Southern" now. That the life before my adoption was over. My identity and nationality before my adoption had been severed. I never felt like I was white and Southern. It wasn't how I was seen in the world. It wasn't how I saw myself. I felt more of a connection to the Latino and Black communities around me. And yet I was forced to hide those friendships and connections.

Early on my parents suggested to me that diversity wasn't necessarily good, and indeed that it was something to fear. It wasn't until I graduated from high school and left for college in New York City that I began to liberate myself from this limiting belief. In the diverse neighborhoods where I lived, I started to see myself in others. I began to form my own perceptions of who I was, as I let go of the early narratives and programming that isolated me and caused a great deal of self-shame.

In New York I felt a sense of ease I'd never felt before. My truth was beginning to emerge. There was no turning back. The city was waking me up and allowing me to excavate a part of myself that had been buried. I was curious about everyone and everything I came in contact with. I spent afternoons exploring museums and hours in the public library reading and writing.

There was that sense of healthy rebellion returning that had been lost since those earlier days as a young girl, picking dandelions in a field. It was like an internal uprising — a necessary step to reach a place of freedom to be me. I was being guided back to a place of knowing. I was growing stronger in the broken places within myself, shoring up the shattered pieces of my story and my biology.

I was beginning to heal in the ways that I needed, and on my terms. For me New York was like a lived experience of DNA testing. Every day I came across someone who initiated an opening to a part of myself that had been dormant for years. The more I came alive, the more my adoptive mother became hurt by the changes in me. She saw my desire to know more of my biology as a criticism of her parenting. "What did I ever do so wrong to make you feel this need to search?" she would ask.

This was my mother's protective response to her own sense of loss, the loss of the girl she wanted to believe I was, as I emerged into a young woman who was reconnecting with herself and search-ing for her true identity. I think it's very important for adoptive parents to grasp that they can't control their adoptee's true nature. Nor should they want to. Moreover, it's vital for adoptive parents to realize that their child can be happy in their present and still want to know more about their past. Adoptees can hold space for both.

Through DNA testing or any other kind of search, adoptees aren't necessarily looking to be embraced back into their biologi-cal families or expecting deep and long relationships with their bio family members. What they do desire — and what is a basic human right to be honored — is the knowledge of their biological identity and the hope that some pieces of medical history might also be made available to them.

The adoptee's search for their biological identity can be lonely. At the end of the day, no one can make the search decisions for the adoptee but the adoptee. It's their individual walk. It's so important for adoptees to be seen, listened to, and allowed to ask questions that can help support them in this often confusing and complicated process of self-discovery. As those who love adoptees, we can tell them that we understand and honor their journey of self-knowing and self-inclusion as they welcome in and reconnect to the places within that were once banished. We can ask them, and we should ask them, how they are doing and what kinds of support they need as they discover more of who they are.

Beyond DNA tests and genealogical research, I have seen and experienced just how important it is for international and transracial adoptees to be offered mirrors of their biological and cultural backgrounds. These parts of who the adoptee is should be celebrated, highlighted, and incorporated into daily life as they grow and develop their sense of identity and self. One cannot erase and should never want to erase an adoptee's internal tapestry because it connects them to their brilliant and beautiful ancestral line.

Cultural events and groups, learning the language of origin, travel and exploration, and books on heritage and diversity can help younger adoptees to feel a little less banished inside as they grow into adults who can make their own decisions about their self-discovery and reconnection to their roots. These things can also be hugely beneficial to adult adoptees beginning or continuing their journey of reconnection and reclamation. I believe that adoptees need to always honor what they feel is best for them as they seek avenues of healing and of coming home to themselves.

A Personal Story of Ancestral Healing

Just a few months ago I was in Sedona, Arizona, and booked a session of somatic healing therapy, a type of body-centered therapy, based on neurobiological research, that illuminates the connection between brain and body. Research has shown that there are twice as many nerves going from the body to the brain as from the brain to the body. What this means is that the body informs the brain. Indeed, the body keeps the score.

In addition to talk therapy, somatic healing therapy uses mind-body exercises and other physical techniques to boost a person's physical and emotional well-being. For adoptees, somatic therapy uses the mind-body connection as an avenue to help us heal from adoption trauma. This therapy session in Sedona was a source of profound insight for me.

I was at a women's retreat and had become intensely aware that I was being called to lead my biological ancestors to a collective healing. I mentioned earlier in this book that healing is ancestral work. What we heal for ourselves, we heal for our entire family line — past, present, and future. What is not healed is passed on to future generations. I had such a strong sensation, while in Sedona, of being frozen inside generational trauma. I was experiencing intense headaches and a shooting pain on my left side that traveled down from my neck and into the arch of my left foot.

The somatic therapy practitioner sat me down and moved me through a series of discovery questions as she led a conversation about my concerns. I explained that I was feeling a heaviness in my body and a sense of anxiety. I shared with her my story of adoption loss and the pain of those lingering feelings of banished biology and history.

At one point the therapist had me stand and envision my biological family — both paternal and maternal — standing in front of me, starting with my first parents and then moving back through the generations. The therapist first had me speak directly to my first parents. Through my tears, I told them that losing them through adoption had been a deep trauma. I added that I was not wired for this kind of early disconnection — no one is! I was suffering in that moment and needed to find a way out of the pain.

I then envisioned my ancestral line moving back, from my first parents to my bio grandparents and beyond. In a long line, I envisioned them all standing before me. I forgave them for the trauma that had been passed on to me. I told them that I was so sorry that they had suffered, too. I asked them to release this trauma so that I could move forward in my life and assist the next generation to live free from the pain. I told them all that I loved them.

Then, when I was ready, I turned my back to my ancestors — not to ignore them but to lead them. I imagined a line of my people standing there with their hands on the shoulders of the person in front of them. I imagined my first parents with their hands on my shoulders. The energy I felt was nothing short of miraculous. I cried as I experienced the ancestral love and support that was buoying me up from behind. I told those standing behind me that I was ready to lead them forward. I was ready to lead my life forward as well. It was a transformational moment that moved me from a place of suffering to a place of healing connection and light.

I left that somatic healing session headache free and with no lingering pain on the left side of my body. I felt lighter and more at ease. I felt loved and more deeply connected to the biology of who I am. I felt folded back into my ancestral blanket. Just writing about that moment makes me smile. I share this experience as an example of another alternative therapeutic technique that can support adoptees in freeing those places within that have felt banished for so long. I think it's vital that, as adoptees, we stay open to alternative modalities of healing and that we choose for ourselves whatever methods — traditional, alternative, or a combination of the two — that feel in alignment with what we need: mind, body, and soul.

REFRAMING EXERCISE
Walking Ancestral Meditation

This reframing exercise will direct you to take a walk. I want you to dive in to this exercise, call on your biological ancestors, and lead them as you walk. I love to walk, and I have had some of my most profound and moving meditative moments and breakthroughs within walking meditation. Yes, you can meditate while you walk; just keep your beautiful eyes open!

The healing benefits of walking are tremendous as you bring body, mind, and spirit in sync, whether you're walking in a local park, in the city, on a remote hiking trail, or inside your home – a mindfulness walk helps promote clearer thinking and self-connection. I believe it greatly supports you along the path of healing. In fact, many of my coaching clients have taken to walking, anywhere from ten to sixty minutes a day, in order to relieve stress and connect to their thoughts, feelings, and creative places within. I'm a big believer in walking at least ten thousand steps a day for overall health. You don't have to start with that, but it can certainly be a goal.

This specific walking ancestral meditation will help you to reset the programming that suggests that we, as adoptees, cannot access our own miraculous biology. Walking and envisioning your ancestors with you can help you reconnect to those places within yourself – those parts of your biology that have felt banished and pushed away.

While this is called a walking ancestral meditation, you can also experience this meditation with any movement that is available to you. If you have a physical disability or if you can't leave home at this time, you can still close your eyes and visualize yourself walking and calling on your ancestors to join you.

This walking meditation can take as long as you'd like, but I do suggest a ten- to twenty-minute walk, as a minimum, as you begin this practice. My walks are normally thirty minutes, sometimes forty-five minutes, two to four times a day – and you can build up to this time if you choose. I often find that I don't want to stop my walking ancestral meditation because it's such an enriching and rewarding experience.

During your walking meditation, you can play your favorite soothing music, or you can choose simply to listen to the sounds of nature around you. If the weather outside is not agreeable, you can walk indoors. You can use a treadmill; just make sure that you create a soothing setting that helps support your sense of peace and comfort. If you haven't taken part in a walking meditation before, that's okay. I ask you to stay open, lean in to the moment, and play.

As you begin your walk, notice what is around you. Let your five senses guide you. Let any thought go that does not connect you to presence. Breathe in what feels good. Breathe out what does not. Receive on the inhale, release on the exhale. Clear the way for a deep encounter.

Keep walking at a pace that feels comfortable and comforting. This is not a race that needs your competitive edge. I want you to soften, open, and experience your feelings as you walk.

Now call on your ancestors to join you. If you know any of their names, say those names out loud or quietly to yourself – whatever feels most natural to you. You'll often find me walking and speaking the names of Cecilia, Eva, Gwyneth, Julielma, and more. These are the names of my ancestors that I have learned through my research. If you don't have that kind of information, that's okay, too. You can call on your ancestors in whatever way feels good and right to you. Names may even come to you as you are walking. Consider these insights as a clue – be a super observer of the information that comes to you and through you.

Ask your ancestors to stay with you on your walk. You can say something like, "I take this time to move my body. I call on my ancestors to walk with me. I am followed and surrounded by the generations that have come before me." As you walk, notice the sensations in your body. Feel the energy of your ancestors as you move. Feel those parts within you that once felt banished start to come alive.

This is an opportunity to reconnect and reclaim. It's also an occasion for noticing what I call points of grace along the way — little signs like a butterfly, a beautiful flower standing alone, or clouds floating by in the shape of something you love. How might these points of grace be connecting you more deeply to those who came before you? How might they be signaling to you that you are guided and loved? Continue to be super observant within this walking meditation, and allow the points of grace along the way to awaken you to new parts of you that are influenced by your miraculous ancestral line.

See if you can identify what aspects of your biology have felt most exiled. Allow all the feelings coming up for you as you walk. It's safe to feel these things. It's also safe to speak these things. As I did in my somatic healing therapy session, feel free to speak to the energy of your ancestors. Ask them to help you release whatever is holding you back. Ask them to renew and reignite within you the biology that has been passed down through the generations. Let those places come alive! With every step you take, free up those places.

Again, keep walking and communicating with those who have come before you, either out loud or in silent imaginative contemplation. Make this walking ancestral meditation your own. Allow the exiled places to step forward. Confide in those places. What has the exiling of these parts of you felt like? What does it feel like to begin reigniting those parts of who you are? Keep talking. Keep walking. Keep breathing. Keep feeling. Continue conversing with your ancestors as you move.

When you are through with your walking ancestral meditation, try journaling or dictating on your phone any thoughts, sensations, or messages that came through to you. I urge you to make this walking meditation a weekly, if not daily, practice. I want you to get in the habit of feeling that you are guided and supported by a loving ancestral line. The truth is, you are!

It's amazing that we have DNA testing and other ways of researching our biology and history as adoptees. We also possess a wealth of information within us that has been passed down through the generations. I have been practicing this walking ancestral meditation for quite some time. When I walk, I call on my ancestors to walk with me, to speak to me, and to speak through me. This practice of walking ancestral meditation has reminded me of my deep connection to my biology and to my ancestral story. It's all within me. It's all within you. I hope you'll practice this simple and gentle meditation as often as you need. Happy walking!

In chapter 8 we'll look at a pain point that comes up often for the adoptees I coach. This pain point has been a major struggle in my own life as well. Yet it's one that I've come to more clearly understand, effectively address, and ultimately heal — the pain of pleasing others versus pleasing the self.

This pain point can manifest in a variety of ways that can be detrimental to the adoptee's overall sense of well-being. Together we'll identify ways that you may be people-pleasing in order to stay safe and be loved. We'll look at ways to shift out of any patterns that are not serving you. I look forward to the work ahead as we move through chapter 8.

Adoptee Affirmation

I can feel a deep connection to my biology at any time.
I am surrounded and guided by my powerful ancestral line.

Chapter Eight

The Pitfalls of Performance

The Pain of Pleasing Others versus Pleasing the Self

"It doesn't feel good to me, but I'll do it anyway if it makes them happy." These words bring tears to my eyes as I write them. I said these words to myself countless times while growing up adopted. I know just how much these words hurt and how small you can feel when this is the messaging in your head, day in and day out.

I didn't know this for a very long time, but I know it now: people-pleasing is a trauma response that, at its core, is rooted in a lack of self-value. When adoptees struggle to value their own desires and needs, they may look for external validation. They can become caught in a pattern of doing things that others want them to do in order to receive their approval and acceptance.

Freeing Ourselves from the Role of Pleaser

It's painful to feel that you have to please others even if that means hurting and disappointing yourself. I believe, without a doubt, that people-pleasing is a form of self-punishment. It's impossible for the adoptee to do what feels right for them when they're continually focused on doing what feels right for everyone else. There are so many pitfalls to feeling as if you have to perform for love, acceptance, and validation. It's been my experience that people-pleasing opens the door for others to take advantage. It's hurtful. It's harmful.

Yet adoptees often find themselves playing the role of pleasers. As children they may perform the roles they believe will keep them safe from rejection — roles like that of the perfect child, the grateful kid, the straight-A student, and the happy little camper. In adults these roles may look like those of the overcommitter, the yes person, or the everyone-else-first person. The adoptee may appear to be the nicest human in the world because they never say no. They anticipate your needs and go over and beyond to keep everyone around them happy. But their continued self-sacrifice comes with a heavy cost.

Chronic people-pleasing can lead to a lack of self-care as the adoptee tends to others at the expense of their own well-being. This dynamic can lead to resentment as the adoptee, over time, feels more and more taken advantage of and underappreciated. People-pleasing can lead to increased feelings of anxiety, stress, and depression as the adoptee juggles more demands than they can handle or more requests than are reasonable.

As for me, I had a long-held limiting belief that it was always better to make others happy. I easily sacrificed my own happiness. I often gave, both physically and emotionally, what I didn't want or have to give. I felt so void of value that I was willing to suspend my own happiness, and sometimes my own safety, just to make someone else feel good. They felt good, I felt bad. Time and time again, it was a very poor trade.

I believed that pleasing others over pleasing myself was a show of love, but it was quite the opposite. People-pleasing was a lack of self-love on daily display. As I look back on that version of me, I see a person still trying to answer the question, *Why did my first parents leave?* I could never arrive at a clear answer, and so my work, as I saw it, was to keep myself safe within my adoptive world by keeping everyone else satisfied.

I constantly apologized for things that weren't my fault. I felt responsible for everyone's emotions, good and bad. I avoided conflict even when I desperately wanted to stand up for myself. I said yes when inside I was screaming no. Each time I put myself in these positions, I made myself smaller and smaller. I felt ashamed and increasingly misunderstood.

The adoptees I coach through pain point number 7, the pain of pleasing others versus pleasing the self, come to me with the hurt of never feeling truly accepted and embraced by their adoptive family. They don't feel they can ever do enough to win their parents' full love and approval, even as adults. Yet they keep trying. And this unconscious behavior pattern extends into other relationships. It's vital for the adoptee to become conscious of the pleasing patterns that may be hurting them. In order to do this, it's imperative that they go beneath the pleasing in order to excavate the pain.

Joanna and Hillary: Trained to Please

Like me, Joanna grew up in a home with an alcoholic adoptive parent. She came to me with intense people-pleasing tendencies. "I feel like I'm a 20 on a scale of 10! I was always the perfect student. I was the natural-born leader in everyone's eyes. I was the supportive and generous one. I could handle anything and seem pretty much unfazed by it all. I was the kid who threw out my dad's bottles of booze before I left for school. I'd then slip my backpack on and head out of the door like it was completely normal. This was my mom's daily request of me, and I did it, faithfully, because it pleased her. It gave her hope that my dad might not drink anymore. It was a short-lived respite from her reality. She could believe, for a moment, that dad didn't drink because the bottles had been removed from the house."

I asked Joanna to go back to that time when she threw out those bottles and begin to excavate the feelings that were underneath and hidden away. She told me that although she seemed unfazed on the outside, she always felt anger on the inside that this was her daily chore, no matter how she felt about it. She didn't want to do it but was afraid to say no because she risked losing her mother's love and approval if she did.

Through our time together, Joanna excavated more of the feelings buried beneath those people-pleasing tendencies that started so many years ago. She began to see her perfectionist role as a desperate need to prove her worth. She recognized the role of the natural-born leader and her need to be in charge as a way to avoid her relinquishment trauma and her feeling that no one was there for her. She began to recognize her role as extreme supporter of everyone else as a way to hide the self-sabotage that was happening inside her. She could move through difficult situations seemingly unfazed because, for so long, she'd diminished her own feelings in order to disregard her deep, deep pain. "I'm not sure if I play out these roles consciously or unconsciously," she said.

I believe that chronic people-pleasing, for the adoptee, is often an unconscious behavior pattern and also an unintentional one initiated by outside forces. Sit with this thought for a moment: adoptees may be unintentionally influenced to become people-pleasers. Consider that once adoptees have lost their first mother, they work exhaustingly hard to win the love of their next mother. They strive to keep in line and always measure up so that they can be in their new mother's good graces. This behavior pattern is not meant to be deceptive. It's the adoptee's brain running the show. It's their survival mechanism on high alert.

The tricky part is that these people-pleasing traits are highly valued in our culture. The adoptee people-pleaser is seen as someone who serves and may even characterize themselves as a server. I'm not saying that showing up for others is a bad thing; however, it can be inwardly destructive if the adoptee's true sense of self is damaged in the process.

Hillary is an adoptee who came to me feeling trapped in the role of peacekeeper when disagreements occurred within her friend group at college. She often became pulled into the middle of drama, and it was causing her a great deal of stress. She saw herself as a person who always shows up for her friends, no matter what. The challenge for Hillary was that this role of perpetual peacekeeper was causing her to feel mentally and emotionally exhausted. She was also feeling more and more frustrated and a little resentful when she perceived her friends as not showing up for her in the same way. She gave herself a score of an 8 on the scale of 1 to 10 in this pain point category.

I asked Hillary where she thought her need to be a peacekeeper originated. "Well, I am the oldest in my family. My parents adopted me because they couldn't have kids of their own. After I was adopted, my mom surprisingly got pregnant with twins. I think it was hard for her to have that many kids in a short amount of time. As I got a little older, I did a lot of peacekeeping between my younger siblings. When they argued, I'd be there to handle the fuss even if I felt stressed out about doing it. My mom always seemed pleased when I stepped in. I wanted to please her."

Pleasing her mother made Hillary feel safe. It also made her feel loved and accepted in her family unit. As a young adult, she'd unconsciously carried the role of peacekeeper into her friendships because she thought it offered her the same love and acceptance that she had desired from her mother. But deep down, something else was going on. I asked Hillary to close her eyes, breathe deeply, and begin to feel the sensations she experiences when she's in peacekeeping mode.

Hillary described an early sense of feeling threatened that her mother might not want her after having biological twins. "I felt like peacekeeping was a way to prove my worth, but the responsibility of keeping the peace between my two siblings was too much. I wanted to stop playing that role, but I couldn't because I was afraid of being sent back if I did. I guess maybe I felt like I could easily be replaced by my younger siblings. I was fearful that if I didn't keep the peace between my siblings and help my mom out in this way, then I wouldn't make the cut."

These were insightful words coming from a keenly intelligent young woman. I asked Hillary if she might consider that the peacekeeping pattern she'd fallen into years ago might really be a people-pleasing pattern. If she kept pleasing her mom, through keeping the peace between her siblings, then she would be safe and loved — even if the pleasing made Hillary feel bad inside. Hillary had been ditching her true feelings and playing an inauthentic role, for years, in order to feel safe and treasured by her mother.

The same pattern had followed Hillary into her young adult life and college friendships. She found it difficult to form friendships that were authentic and not dependent on her continuing the role of peacekeeper. Hillary's friends seemed pleased that she was their go-to girl to keep the peace when drama hit in the friend group. Yet Hillary was exhausted from this people-pleasing role that she'd been playing since childhood. It had become a barrier to her accessing places within herself that felt healthy, authentic, and true.

As adoptees, when we continually put the feelings and wants of others before our own, we lose ourselves. I worked with both Hillary and Joanna on ways to shift those people-pleasing tendencies and to step out of the inauthentic roles they'd been playing for years. I'll review those steps with you as we move deeper into this chapter.

First, though, I want to acknowledge that sometimes it's hard to look at our own points of pain, as adoptees. I understand just how hard it can be! You are so courageous to be doing this work because it's challenging to stare into the pain. It's kind of like looking directly into the sun — you may fear getting burned. But look we must. In our own timing and in ways that feel safe, we can explore these pain points within ourselves. I don't believe you get burned by being brave enough to look into the places where pain has you coiled up and trapped. One thing I know for sure: when you look at these places, you will begin to see the light. Clarity comes. Truths emerge. Healing begins.

I also want to reiterate that the adoptee experience is a lifelong journey. Please don't think that you have to heal in a day. It doesn't work that way. Healing takes time, plus actionable steps. As we learn to trust and love ourselves more, we can begin to choose the healing modalities that feel right to us. And that's going to look different for each adoptee. Trust what you need! As hard as healing can be, I hope you will envision and get excited about the person waiting for you on the other side.

—⁓—

ADOPTEE AWAKENING: *Adoptees can't heal if they keep pretending that they aren't hurt.*

Please sit with this awakening for a moment. When adoptees are caught in a pattern of people-pleasing it can be very difficult to sense their own needs. Remember, this mode of behavior is centered on survival. It's a stress response — one focused on pleasing in order to avoid conflict. As long as adoptees are focused on avoiding potential conflict with others, they are more prone to avoiding their own needs and, indeed, their own points of pain. They may be reluctant to let go of this behavior pattern because it has offered them a sense of security in the past. And this reluctance can delay their healing. As adoptees, it's vital that we learn to show up for ourselves — first and foremost. No one should feel the need to perform a role in order to be loved.

The Origin of My Pleasing Pattern

I want to share a personal story because it goes back to the moment when I had a conscious childhood realization that in order to stay safe from rejection, and in order to be loved, I would need to please everyone around me. The resulting behavior patterns that followed me for years were unconscious but initiated in a moment that remains a vivid memory for me.

I can clearly recall the feeling of needing to please my adoptive mother in all that I did, even if her request made me feel bad inside. I was her shining light, and I was to fill the hole in her heart left by my father's alcohol abuse. Failing to meet my mother's many expectations left me feeling defective. I felt like a failure, and that feeling fed into my limiting belief that I had failed my first parents and somehow caused their rejection of me.

The pressure of pleasing others was ever present for me. I felt constantly at risk of being sent back, which was a very similar feeling to what Hillary had experienced while growing up and is a very real fear among many adoptees. When you've been removed from your first life, what's to stop you from being removed again?

That threat was always looming in my mind from as far back as I can remember. I recall the moment from childhood when I had the vivid realization that I was expected to please. When my family would visit my maternal adoptive grandmother, I'd walk up the front porch steps and brace myself for the door hinges to squeak loudly and announce our arrival. My visits to her home were normally filled with my desire to leave — it wasn't the average joy-filled trip to Grandma's house. My grandmother was married to a financially successful businessman. He was husband number three.

Something about this man made me very uncomfortable. Even as a girl of six or seven, I had a gut feeling — an internal sense of warning — to stay a few feet away from him. One evening, when we were ending a visit, my mother urged me to go and give my "grandfather" a kiss goodbye on the cheek. I hesitated as if to say no. It was the first time that I'd ever openly challenged my mother's directive, and it was an awkward moment. I felt anxiety in the pit of my stomach and it made me nauseous.

Mom's expectation of me was clear. I was to do what she said and be a respectful granddaughter. Only this man was not a grandfather to me. I barely knew him. He scared me. I stared at him with my big, dark eyes. My knees were trembling. My grandmother's husband sat at the opposite end of the dinner table and waited for me to come close. He was eating corn on the cob — my favorite — and the kernels were flying from the corners of his mouth. Bits of corn landed on the table like tiny meteors crashing down to earth. The way he ate was repulsive. I started to cry.

"Go on, Michelle." Mom was nudging me forward. As she nudged, I pushed back. For a few short minutes, we played a game of tug-of-war. Then Mom pushed me a little harder toward the table. I stood there looking up as this man kept eating. *Maybe he doesn't see me standing here*, I thought to myself. A split second of relief. Then a tiny piece of kernel hit my jaw. I wiped it away, sickened.

My grandmother's husband looked down at me and said, "Place a kiss right here on my cheek." I could see a shiny residue of butter on the spot where he pointed. I leaned away and looked at my mom. She was annoyed. "Michelle, give a kiss goodbye. We have to be leaving soon."

Everyone in the room was staring at me. There was no way out. I was expected to make good on my mother's demands. I was expected to please her. I also really wanted to please her. I closed my eyes as the buttery, wrinkled cheek of my grandmother's husband moved closer to my mouth. I knew we'd made contact when the taste of butter was on my lips. Tears were streaming down my face. I looked at my mother and said, "Can I go now?" She nodded that I could and then gave me a good-girl pat on the shoulder. I ran out of my grandmother's house, blowing through her doorway and down the front porch steps.

The tone had been set — I was a girl expected to please my mother. On top of that, I craved her approval and affection. I considered my own feelings as less worthy of respect and attention. I didn't value my voice. On that day, I disconnected from my gut wisdom. That moment set a precedent that my role was to please others, even if it hurt me. The consequences of not pleasing were far too risky. I truly believed that I would lose my mother's love and be sent back to foster care if I failed to please her and everyone around me. I would be seen as bad.

It wasn't until I started doing the deep work of facing my own pain points, as an adoptee, that I realized that the people-pleasing role I'd played for so long was actually seeded in that ordeal at my grandmother's house. And that this moment had set a precedent for my relationships with others as I grew.

REFLECTION EXERCISE
Pinpointing When the Pleasing Pattern Began

For this reflection exercise, I'd like you to take some time and journal on the following questions. These are the same questions that I've moved through along my own journey of healing my people-pleasing tendencies. They are the same questions that both Joanna and Hillary moved through. Again, take your time. There's no rush. Be honest with yourself. Be tender with what comes up for you.

1. Where are you on a scale of 1 to 10 for pain point number 7, the pain of pleasing others versus pleasing yourself?

2. When do you first remember feeling you had to perform for and please someone else even when

it made you feel bad or sad? What happened? Who was there? What did they say? What did they do? Go back and track the moment when you re- member having a conscious thought of: I need to please, no matter what. Do you remember a voice saying you needed to please in order to be loved, accepted, embraced? For Joanna, this moment was when she started throwing out her father's bottles of booze in order to satisfy her mother's request and give herself a sense of temporary relief. For Hillary, it was when she became the peacekeeper in her family in order to ease her mother's parent- ing stress. For me, it was that moment in my grand- mother's house.

3. How might this moment, for you, still be triggered today and cause an unconscious pattern of pleas- ing others over pleasing yourself? Are you putting the needs of others before your own? Are you dis- regarding your own views of the world – stepping out of alignment with your own values – in order to receive approval from others?

4. Are you caught up in a *no-matter-what* or *even-if* thought pattern? Do you hear a voice in your head saying it's better to please others, no matter what? Do you believe that it's best to please others even if it leaves you feeling stripped of self-worth? What thoughts or images go through your mind when you are triggered to please others in a way that feels unhealthy for you? What actions do you take as a result? What do you say or do?

5. Ask yourself what an alternative behavior would look like for you, one that offered you the best pos- sible outcome, in moments when you lean toward

pleasing someone else over honoring your own desires and needs. What actions could bring you more in alignment with your values, no matter the outside influence? Go deep, and remember that the answer is within you. All that you need to shift those people-pleasing tendencies is found within you, right here and right now.

Those around you can often sniff out a people-pleaser and may take advantage of the fact that you place others' needs before your own. As adults, establishing healthy boundaries is key. A first solid step toward that end is saying no — without feeling like you owe an explanation. If you want to explain your decision further, you can simply say: "This just doesn't feel right for me at this time." Practice saying this in front of a mirror. Feel the energy of speaking your truth and saying no to the situations that don't feel right for you. It's like building muscle memory — the more we strengthen that part of us, the easier it is to call on it when needed.

Whether you scored yourself at a 2 or a 10 on the scale for this pain point, there are discoveries to be made that will help lessen the people-pleasing behavior patterns that may be keeping you from living on your own terms each and every day. As an adoptee, you are allowed to put your happiness first. Take that in! You are allowed to love yourself in this way. Boundaries are beautiful. They are a form of self-care and a reminder of your undeniable self-worth.

REFRAMING EXERCISE
Joy, the Inner Child, and You

Many adult adoptees share that their people-pleasing tendencies began in childhood. As I stated earlier in this chapter, the loss of their first mother can cause adoptees to exhaust themselves trying to please their next mother. They may feel like they don't have a choice but to please others before pleasing themselves. The thought of another rejection is far too scary. This was the case for me and for my coaching clients Joanna and Hillary.

Early in our lives, we were constantly watching for ways in which we could please our adoptive mothers, and everyone else around us, in order to ensure the love and connection we longed for after losing our first mothers. These behavior patterns, which followed us into adulthood, were unconscious and ultimately unhealthy. Breaking the patterns would require us to reframe our focus. Instead of being hypervigilant and constantly tuned in to what would please others, we had to begin to ask ourselves, *What pleases me?*

This reframing exercise will help you focus on what brings you joy instead of placing your sole focus on the opinions and reactions of others. Ultimately, the continued practice of this exercise will support you in speaking your mind in all situations and understanding that you do have a choice. Indeed, you have a voice! You may even begin to celebrate and honor all the unique things that make you who you are. Remember, when you're busy pleasing others all the time, it is impossible to live authentically. I want you to live an authentic and joy-filled life!

You see, we can't control how other people view us. We can't control whether they will love us. We can, however, control how we view ourselves and how we love ourselves. At the end of the day, it's this self-opinion and self-love that truly matter.

1. Choose a childhood photo of yourself and place it on the mirror in your bathroom or somewhere that you're sure to go to, daily. This should be a photo from your childhood that brings you a sense of joy when you see it.

2. Every day connect with the child in the photo and speak with her about all the things she loves to do. My inner child reminds me that she loves spending time with horses and dogs and taking walks in nature. She reminds me of her love of travel and of meeting new people in new places. She reminds me of the great comfort she's always felt when writing, and of the peace she feels while watching a sunset over the mountains.

3. Ask this child what she most likes to create. Is it paintings, songs, fun meals, magical moments? Does your inner child love writing poetry or music? Does she love to laugh? Document all that comes to you.

4. Now dialogue on the three to five things that you most like about each other. What qualities do you see in her that inspire you and help you to remember a truer version of yourself? What qualities in you can help her to heal the hurts from her childhood?

5. Now it's time to make a promise that when those people-pleasing tendencies sneak in, you will think of this child and speak up for her — and know that in the process you are speaking up for you, too. There is no loss to be found when you are speaking your truth and focusing on what matters most to you. Stand up for yourself, no matter what. Stand up for your inner child. This is how you discover an aligned sense of self and how you become more willing to honor your truth.

Write these responses down, or record them on your phone. Keep them close, and revisit them as you continue this dialogue with your inner child. The more you practice this reframing exercise and move from being a super pleaser of others to being a super observer of what you need – and what your inner child needs – the more clarity you will have about what you stand for.

Joanna and Hillary speak to their inner child, in the mirror, every day. Joanna has learned that her truest joy is found in her imperfections, and she's now the natural-born leader of herself, of her needs and desires. She's become an extreme supporter of herself first, and that's changed everything. Joanna's pain point is no longer a 20 on a scale of 10. As of this writing, she's at a 6.

Hillary now focuses on being a peacekeeper for herself and her life. She knows that speaking her truth is the way to protect and cultivate peace within. She no longer has the knee-jerk reaction to jump in and make the peace in her friend group or within her family. Both women have learned to set healthy boundaries and to say no, with grace and dignity. They have come to realize, just as I have, that they can't be everything to everyone. It's best to be true to yourself. That's a decision we can all live with and celebrate.

In the next chapter, we'll explore pain point number 8, the pain of a lack of transparency and acceptance. We'll look at the vital importance of transparency, acceptance, and community along this journey as adoptees. We'll consider how the tangled parts of our stories may just hold the clues to our unique calling as individuals.

Adoptee Affirmation

I am a pleaser of self.
It is okay to please me, to speak up for me, and to stay true to what matters most to me.

Chapter Nine

Realigning with the Light of Transparency and Acceptance

A doptees ache to live in alignment with their truth. Voice by voice and truth by truth, adoptees are committing to real change because they simply cannot be silenced and censored anymore. They're mobilizing and moving toward the light of transparency.

In the dictionary the definition of the word *transparency* is "the quality of being transparent — something that allows for the passage of light." I pondered this definition, as I'm a big believer in light. I believe in the power of our inner light and in living in such a way that promotes the shining of our luminous energy. I believe that our light is our gift to the world. And I believe that every adoptee possesses their own unique and extraordinary light.

I dimmed my light for a very long time. I felt like I couldn't get back to a place inside myself where my spark was still waiting. My limiting belief was that I couldn't be transparent because, if I was, I might be left with no one. I couldn't be real. I couldn't be me. So I waited in the dark. Perhaps I was waiting for someone to save me, someone to piece back together the crumbled connections of my life as an adoptee — someone to make peace of the pieces.

I discovered, over time, that this someone had to be me — she *was* me! I no longer wanted to live with the lack of transparency looming over me. I desired an abundance of clarity and clearness. I wanted to be clear with myself and with everyone around me. I began to sense the power I possessed to reignite my own flickering flame. I became curious about this flame. It was my life force, and I knew I would need raw transparency to set it ablaze.

Adoptees are ready for raw and real transparency. I hear it and see it every day. As one adoptee recently wrote to me, "Adoptees have been silent for so long. Too long! We haven't been able to be transparent, and so people out there aren't aware of what we've been going through. Thank you for the enlightenment!"

I truly believe that the adoptee community is at a tipping point — a critical threshold — where, voice by voice, we're creating shifts in perception and illuminating truth within the adoption conversation. These shifts are beginning to spread like wildfire and are reflected in the growing conversations and connections being made online as adoptees find each other on a global level. I can say with all certainty that my online adoptee community has been a tremendous source of support, education, and comfort for me. I know this is also the case for many other adoptees. The most healing bit of awareness is the knowing that we are not alone! The shifts being made as adoptees connect aren't meant to destroy but to clear away any debris blocking a more inclusive conversation, one that better supports adoptees both individually and collectively — no matter their age, their experience, or their perspective. If there is one thing I know, with all that I am, it is this: our ability to be real, raw, and transparent about our own human journey as adoptees is what will heal us, free us, and ignite our unstoppable light-filled potential.

Cindy Comes Out of the Fog

When Cindy came to me for coaching, she felt all eight pain points shared in this book on some level, but she quickly realized that the last pain point — a lack of transparency in her life — was likely the root from which all the other pain points had grown. "This is where the emotional turmoil started for me. I couldn't be transparent in my adoptive home, and so I never found a way to accept myself. Everything seemed to crumble from there."

Cindy had only learned of the phrase *coming out of the fog* just a few short months before connecting with me. "I didn't know it was a thing, but it makes sense to me now that I do." Cindy had always known that she was adopted but had grown up in a household where it was never transparently talked about. Adoption, in her words, was a taboo topic — don't ask, don't tell, don't feel, don't be real. She'd spent sixty years in the murky atmosphere of feeling silenced, numbed out emotionally, and disconnected to her authentic inner world. "I had no way to ground myself to anything that felt genuine while I was growing up. It seems like it should have been obvious to my parents that I might have some curiosities or questions about being adopted. Instead, they just ignored it. I learned how to ignore it, too — maybe it was just the times we were living in."

The lack of transparency in Cindy's life had resulted in her losing a sense of self. She felt she had no choice but to lose a part of herself instead of potentially losing those who preferred, consciously or not, that she stay blocked from all the feelings she needed to explore. Cindy lived in a way that felt comfortable for everyone else but her. This unconscious people-pleasing behavior left her feeling disconnected and alone. If she was transparent about what was going on inside her, she risked being rejected. You can see how a lack of transparency was triggering her other points of pain.

Life felt blurry to Cindy. It's was as if she could see the letters on the vision chart but couldn't clearly make them out. Her sense of isolation grew as she was left to wonder, alone, about her bio family and bio story. "I knew that I had other people out there who were connected to me. Obviously, I have a bio family and a first story, but

I truly believed that I'd never be given the eyes to clearly see what it all might mean to me."

Cindy, like so many adoptees, felt forced to bow out of her feelings and to take a sledgehammer to any thoughts about her adoption. She described the sensation as being like an involuntary urge to smash the thoughts to pieces before she was compelled to speak them.

—∽—

ADOPTEE AWAKENING: *Self-acceptance requires transparency.*

Please sit with the above adoptee awakening for a moment. How can adoptees fully accept themselves when so many of them have never felt free to be fully transparent with themselves? How can adoptees forge transparent relationships when the examples, within their adoptive world, have often been ones of concealment and obscurity?

Here's the bottom line: transparency, even when it's painful, even when it does not fall on welcoming ears, is absolutely necessary. It's vital that adoptees be real and raw with themselves and with others; otherwise, they may find themselves disconnecting and disengaging. They may even feel irreversibly disempowered.

For years I believed that adoption was my weakness, that it was my kryptonite. I believed that being adopted was an embarrassment and that it reduced my worth and rendered me powerless. I didn't want to talk about my adoption because I didn't want to show those emotional cards. Everyone around me spoon-fed the narrative that adoption was all shine. I knew better, but swallowing that narrative seemed safer at the time than chewing on the truth. It also felt less risky because openly expressing my real emotions was normally met with disappointment from my mother and a sense that I had somehow done something wrong.

I became less and less transparent with myself and with others. I couldn't find a path toward self-acceptance. I didn't see any way to embrace or speak out loud my broken and imperfect story. And, like Cindy, I avoided feeling the pain. I avoided claiming the pain. I avoided naming the pain.

Yet the cure for the pain is found in the pain. When you bring light to your pain, it too will become light. As adoptees, we need to fully feel our emotions. We need to become open and honest and reach a point where our unique self — including the adoptee part of who we are — is seen, heard, and acknowledged. And this requires transparency.

I mentioned earlier in the book that we adoptees can be pioneers of our lives. We can boldly step into our emotional healing and spiritual awakening, leading our lives forward. We can be "spiritual pioneers," as Eckhart Tolle puts it: "Spiritual pioneers: people who are reaching a point where they become capable of breaking out of inherited collective mind-patterns that have kept humans in bondage to suffering for eons." Breaking out of the inherited narrative and collective thought patterns that keep adoptees from thriving begins with transparency.

Through transparency adoptees can grow as individuals and as a community, as they pick up each piece of their story, examine it, and reshape it into something new and empowering. They can begin to embrace and accept themselves, as well as all the moments of their adoption journey. Adoptees can begin to reframe and renew the meaning of those moments for themselves.

I hear from adoptees weekly who say they've just shared their story for the first time on a podcast, before a live audience, or in a blog post. They tell me how empowering it is to finally speak the truth. They say that they do it for their fellow adoptees. This sense of service is what motivates adoptees to rise up and be greater than the pain points. It's within this place of growth and contribution that adoptees are finding their own meaningful ways toward leadership.

My coaching client Cindy first revealed the story of her adoptee journey at a gathering during a retreat in Costa Rica. She shared with me that a man sat down at her table and began to share his life story with her. He then asked Cindy about her story. For the first time, she openly shared her adoption journey and the lessons she'd learned thus far about who she is and why she's here. By the end of her sharing, the entire table — with laser-like focus — was homed in on Cindy's story because they'd never really contemplated the complexities of adoption before.

Cindy, through her transparency, had educated others and elevated the adoption conversation by sharing her story openly and honestly. "I spoke for myself and for every adoptee out there. I felt empowered to speak from my heart. I still can't believe that I spoke so freely and honestly. Now that I have, though, I can't imagine moving forward in any other way."

Dealing with Being Adopted

"It's been a crazy life, learning how to monitor my words and my feelings as I deal with being adopted." It is not uncommon for me to hear this kind of pain — rooted in a lack of transparency — coming from the adoptees who request my coaching support. They share just how exhausting it has been for them to manage life as an adoptee.

I wonder what would happen to this beautiful community of souls if we could step away from the moment-to-moment managing of our thoughts and emotions as adoptees and just be honest about our lived experience — without fear of judgment or ridicule. This fear is real. Adoptees often face degrading comments when they speak their stories and perspectives out loud. They are told that they're ungrateful, should have been left in an orphanage, or perhaps not even born at all. American memoirist and activist Maya Angelou once said, "There is no greater agony than bearing an untold story inside you." Adopted or not, every person deserves to give voice to their story without feeling judged, shamed, or diminished. Our story is our humanity. What would the world look like if we could listen to each other even when we don't agree? I imagine it would be much like what Cindy expressed after sitting at that table in Costa Rica and sharing her real adoption story. It would be empowering and transformational.

Each chapter, exercise, meditation, affirmation, and awakening in this book was designed to help you discover soulful ways to express, with transparency and authenticity, your points of pain along this adoptee journey. It is through sharing their stories — scars, flaws, and all — that adoptees will transform the adoption conversation, along with the lives of adoptees near and far. It won't be easy; nothing worthwhile ever is. Yet when we deny our real and very human adoption stories, and the shadow and shine within those stories, we deny our inner champion the chance to emerge. And as I shared in the early pages of this book, I believe that every adoptee is a hero.

Have you ever contemplated that it's not possible to have a *message* without a *mess*? I don't want a perfect, mess-free adoption story. I used to believe that I needed one. I felt really broken knowing that I didn't have the kind of story that was featured in those feel-good adoption articles. I used to share only the parts of my story that made my adoptee journey look glossy and glowing. I didn't want to disappoint, and so I kept the parts that gutted me to myself.

Here's what I've learned: even the best adoption stories hold their messy parts. I want to hear more about those parts because that's where we connect within our humanity. That's how we grow and become more real with ourselves and with each other. It's how we work through the mess and get to the glowing parts. It's in our humanity that we make long-lasting positive change for adoptees, both present and future. Looking at the messy parts of the adoptee experience — bringing those parts into the open — is how we can begin to make the journey better for another generation of adoptees. Share the shine, but please stop denying the shadow where it exists. We need both the shadow and the shine in order to arrive at the fullest value of what it means to be adopted.

I used to hide away because I saw myself as a damaged adoptee with a damaged story. It took time for me to understand that sometimes we're led into the tangled wilderness in order to learn more of who we are and why we're here. I came to understand, through a whole lot of soul searching and deep internal healing work, that the tangled parts of my adoptee journey might just reveal the clues to my unique calling.

—m—

ADOPTEE AWAKENING: *Meaningful connection and a capacity for empathy start with a willingness to transparently share the scars of our adoptee experience.*

Transparency starts within us, but it's also either supported or shut down at home within our adoptive family structure. You'll recall that for Cindy adoption was a taboo topic in her house. This isn't a rare occurrence. Adoptees often express that they weren't allowed to ask questions about their adoption or openly share their feelings while growing up. And since adoption transparency was lacking, there was a loss of connection and trust. The message that Cindy and so many other adoptees receive is that they can't transparently talk about their lives before being adopted — regardless of how short or long the time frame of that first life was.

All too often adult adoptees express that they couldn't openly explore their thoughts about the first families who remained on their minds and in their hearts while growing up. It was difficult — if not impossible — for them to process their feelings in a healthy way in their adoptive households. As a result, it became increasingly tough to embrace and accept themselves and to make meaning of their adoption story.

It's vital that we reframe the rules of adoption and make transparency the bedrock of our conversations and explorations. For adoptees who didn't have that growing up, it's essential that they can begin to process their adoptee experience and safely explore their feelings in ways that align with their needs. Remember, your path to healing doesn't have to look exactly like anyone else's. Trust your inner voice, and follow its lead. Create the healing path that is meant for you.

For adoptive parents, I urge you to create some sacred space in which to talk with your adoptee about their thoughts, feelings, and questions. How can you show them that you support them? How can you honor the life that came before their adoption? How can you create openness about the adoption regardless of how it came about? I often use the acronym OPEN, and I'd like to share it with you here to help you forge more transparent communication with your adoptee. And, for the adult adoptee, you can use this acronym to guide yourself toward more transparent conversation with others and more meaningful inner dialogue.

REFLECTION EXERCISE
OPEN

O is for *offering unconditional love, always*. Frame conversations with your adoptee in a setting of unconditional love. Tell them — speak the words — that your love for them is unconditional. That there is no topic they can't present to you, no topic they are not safe to explore. That there's nothing they could possibly do or say that would end your love for them. When you begin any conversation within this covenant, it softens your approach and opens everyone up to receive. Take off the defensive armor and show up, soul to soul.

P is for *preparing safe spaces* for hearing the adoptee. Where does the adoptee in your life feel most safe? Is it under a favorite tree? Is it in a favorite chair? Is it in their bedroom with a beloved pet or favorite plushy toy in their lap? If the adoptee is older, might the safe space be walking along the beach or sitting together with a warm cup of tea? Might it be while driving in the car and conversing one-on-one? I've had some transformational heart-to-heart conversations with my teen son while sitting in my car at night, after his football practice. Let your adoptee have a voice in selecting whatever safe space helps them open up and be safely held and heard.

E is for *engaging with your child* and never forcing your opinion on them or judging them. Allow your child's truth to emerge. When an adoptee feels forced or pressured to share, they'll likely close up because they no longer feel safe. Now that my kids are in their teens, I've learned ways to engage without closing them off. I ask them this question when they come to me and want to share: "I want to hear everything you have to say, but can we clarify if you want me to just listen, or would you like my perspective and guidance?" It's like filling the space around the conversation with pillows of grace. It creates a softer landing for transparency and loving connection.

N is for *nurturing an atmosphere of "always here and always ready to listen."* It's the stop, drop, and lean in transparency formula. Be in the moment with your adoptee. Be present as they share what's going on in their minds and hearts. Put the phone down. Turn off the TV. Be with your adoptee. Be there. Be ready to listen.

I think as we reflect on and reframe our approaches to the adoption conversation, we can ease the sense that adoptees have of "dealing with being adopted" to a healthier place of openly "feeling being adopted." What a gift we can offer to a younger generation of adoptees as we honor their earliest stories and everyone in those stories. What a gift it is to encourage transparency in sharing their unvarnished thoughts and feelings. It's never too late, as adult adoptees, to give this gift to ourselves as well. We no longer have to simply deal with our experience. Dealing is done from a place of survival. We can feel. We are safe to feel! This is where we begin to heal and to thrive.

I'd also like to offer up this thought: If we are asking adoptees for their transparency, can we also urge adoptive parents, birth parents, and all those who work to support adoptees and foster youth for theirs? Might we consider that each of us carries a wound that is primal and in need of bringing into the light? Might we look at our own triggers and take responsibility for them? Might we see the adoptee as not the only one in need of healing? We all have hurting parts in need of care. No one is made weak by saying that. We are made stronger in our vulnerability. Might we be willing – together – to heal this adoption community and create space for deeper understanding even within opposing conversations? We have to dig deep and talk about what isn't working so that we can find a more holistic approach to adoptee healing. If it takes a village to raise a child, so too does it take a village to heal a child.

We've all been children in need of healing, and often that unhealed child remains within us. As adults it is our responsibility to nurture our inner child back to a place of wholeness. It is hard to give to others what we have yet to give to ourselves. Adoptees deserve whole, healthy, healed parents and adults around them. Adoptees deserve to be whole, healthy, and healed themselves.

REFRAMING EXERCISE
Viewing Transparency in a Whole New Way

The reframing exercise for this chapter holds a simple directive: journal on how you can view transparency in a whole new way. As you journal, please consider these questions as helpful prompts. What has been your relationship to transparency? How have you viewed it in the past? Were transparent conversation and openhearted sharing a part of your household while growing up? In what ways have you had to bury your light because you didn't feel you could be transparent with yourself and with others? How has burying your light affected how you live and love? How can you be more transparent, whether you are an adoptee, adoptive parent, birth parent, or someone who works in the area of adoption? How have your views about transparency and adoption changed? How might reframing your view of transparency transform your life and reignite your light? How can you apply a healthier dose of transparency with yourself and with others? How might transparency lead you toward an acceptance of self that you've yet to realize? How might that self-acceptance positively shift your life, your relationships, and your sense of clarity about your calling and purpose?

Journal as long as you'd like on these questions. Sit in stillness, and listen for the answers to arrive. Give yourself time to receive what wants to come to you. There is no rush.

Transparency asks of us to be still and to allow for the light that is waiting to shine through.

Forgiveness goes hand in hand with healing. In our final chapter, I'd like to guide you through a simple yet profound prayer that I use to clear anything in me that might be blocking my ability to live transparently and from a place of pure love and grace. The prayer is an ancient Hawaiian practice known as Ho'oponopono. I've used this practice for years, and it's radically transformed my life and the lives of the countless adoptees I have had the privilege of coaching. May this prayer of Ho'oponopono be a blessing to you and to all those in your life — past, present, and future.

Adoptee Affirmation

I choose transparency.
I choose to light my path forward with all that is real and true.

Chapter Ten

The Light of Forgiveness
and Clearing Inner Blocks

I love you. I'm sorry. Please forgive me. Thank you. These four simple phrases have transformed my life. I'd like to introduce you to an ancient Hawaiian forgiveness practice that helps to remove the internal blocks and triggers that may be getting in the way of your emotional, mental, and physical freedom. It's simple — profound in its simplicity — and it works. This healing practice is known as Ho'oponopono.

If we dissect this Hawaiian word, it looks like Ho'o means "cause" and *ponopono* means "perfection." The word translates into English simply as "correction." This ancient problem-solving process of reconciliation and forgiveness is done to help something to move back into balance, or to right a wrong. It's been widely used to restore and maintain good family relationships within the Hawaiian culture. This practice is based on the belief that when we clear our inner blocks, the outer world responds.

I first read about this practice in a book called *Zero Limits* by Jim Vitale. The book details the true story of a psychologist who healed an entire ward of mentally ill criminals without ever seeing a single patient. The psychologist would review the files of his patients and, as he did so, he would work on himself through this process of Ho'oponopono. He spoke these four life-altering phrases as he looked through the charts of the patients in the ward. He spoke them inside himself as an offering. He offered these words up to God, the Universe, the divine:

I love you. I'm sorry. Please forgive me. Thank you.

What really happened here? Apparently, when the psychologist looked through the charts of his patients, he felt emotions like embarrassment, rage, anger, guilt, and a variety of other feelings. He was super observant about what was coming up for him as he focused on clearing those places within himself. He wasn't trying to heal the patient; instead, he looked to heal the emotions that the patient was triggering in him. As he healed his emotions he reconnected to spirit — the sacred space of zero limits where anything is possible. Once he arrived at this place of inner peace, the patients responded with healing of their own.

I hope this book has helped you connect to that spiritual place within you, that sacred space of zero limits where anything is possible — awakening limitless truths within yourself, recognizing your vast potential to heal your life, and growing greater than the pain points of the adoptee experience.

When we focus on clearing our internal world, the energy of our external world changes. Where focus goes, energy flows. This practice, which focuses on healing our inner world, can be of great benefit to adoptees.

When you accept total responsibility for everything you notice within yourself, you are in essence saying that some part of you helped to create what you notice. Take that in for a moment. Remember that you are responsible for your own internal garden, just like the young adoptee in Europe you met earlier in this book, who was learning the responsibility of tending to her garden at school. If the garden gets out of balance, the gardener must tend to the soil and clear away what is blocking the garden's ability to heal and to grow.

Taking total responsibility for everything in the soil of our internal garden means that we are ultimately accountable for the healing of every pain point seeded in that soil — every feeling of being unwelcome, every bit of grief, every denial of truth, all the fear of rejection and pain of distrust, all the loss of a banished biology, every people-pleasing tendency, and every moment filled with a lack of transparency. When we, as adoptees, can own these things, we can find the power to heal them. We find the power to nurture peace within us so that our outer world will respond and come back into balance around us.

Through taking responsibility and stating that the negative programming stored in our minds is causing our dis-ease and pain, adoptees acknowledge that this mindset can be reprogrammed and our lives transformed. Adoptees can trust that when they do, the outer world will respond in kind.

What could be more empowering? When we take responsibility for the past and the present, we also take responsibility for the future. The power shifts from them to me. The power to navigate my healing shifts from them to me. The power to create my future shifts from them to me. The power to discover my God-given purpose shifts from them to me. The power to grow greater than the pain points is shifted from them to me.

I love you. I'm sorry. Please forgive me. Thank you.

I say these four phrases when I open my eyes in the morning and before I close my eyes at night. I say them throughout my day and whenever I notice a limiting belief or a bad-feeling thought sneak in. I repeat these words when I feel triggered by something or someone. I speak these words of forgiveness to myself in order to release the shame and blame of my adoptee journey. I whisper these words and forgive the inauthentic behavior patterns that sometimes slip through. I say these four phrases and know that by so doing, I am healing not only myself but also the collective. I say these words and trust that the divine is receiving as I am releasing. Clarity and, yes, transparency arrive.

—⚭—

ADOPTEE AWAKENING: *Memories and triggers are old programs replaying. When adoptees open up to clearing these places within, inspiration — divine messaging — comes through. The adoptee's internal world is transformed, and their outer world responds.*

The Passing of My Parents

Both my adoptive parents passed away in 2016, exactly one month apart. When they were gone I felt abandoned all over again. It's as if the sensations of being left by my first mother and father had been stored inside my body and the death of my adoptive mother and father had caused all that emotion and uncertainty to come rushing back in.

When my adoptive father died, I was on FaceTime with him from California. He could no longer speak, and his breath was shallow. As my dad looked at me, I could tell that he wanted to say, "I'm sorry." Through my tears, I told Dad that it was okay and that I wanted him to rest. I began speaking, softly, the words of Ho'oponopono. With my hands over my heart I whispered, *I love you. I'm sorry. Please forgive me. Thank you.*

Nothing else mattered but for me to offer up to the divine all the brokenness that still resided inside me so that I could hold, tenderly and compassionately, the broken parts of my father as he took his final breaths. As I whispered the words of Ho'oponopono, it came to me that I had, for so long, been triggered by my father, not only because of his drinking but also because he, too, had lost a dad as a child. That bruised and broken place of loss within me was heightened around my adoptive father, my own sense of anger and insecurity triggered.

As my father lay there dying, I saw him as a little boy who had lost his own father at age eleven. For the first time, I saw my dad as an innocent child who never had the tools to heal. It's why he drank and lashed out in anger toward me and my mother. He was angry with himself and with the disappointments and losses in his life. He didn't know where to place his anger, so it spilled over onto us.

There is no denying that my father's actions hurt me while I was growing up, yet Ho'oponopono helped me find a way to clear my programming and to forgive. Within that place of forgiveness, I was set free, and so was my dad. Those taking care of my father told me that his passing, among all the hundreds they had witnessed, was the most peaceful they'd ever seen. I didn't do that. The divine did.

Although my dad knew that he could never go back and erase his actions toward me when I was growing up, he had been an incredibly loving grandfather to my kids. He loved them with all that he was. Dad had stopped drinking later in his life, and to this day my children fondly remember the doting love of their grandfather. The practice of Ho'oponopono has helped me to remember that man, the loving grandfather, and to hold a space of love for the little boy inside my dad who for so much of his life felt alone and lost.

When my adoptive mother died, four weeks after my father, she did so with grace and an unwavering faith. I was there by my adoptive mother's side when she passed away. I know that she loved me, but I don't think my mother ever quite got me. She had a vision of who she wanted me to be. Trying to be that daughter just wasn't sustainable for me; it wasn't my authentic self. I had to become all that I needed to be. I had to stop chasing the little girl held in my mother's dreams. I had to honor my first me because it was that little girl that I needed to show up for and reclaim. I became a woman on the day I decided to step into my own vision for my life.

My adoptive mother and I never had a chance to be fully transparent about my adoption. She didn't recognize adoption as loss. I needed to claim those places of loss within me so that I could move forward and heal. I do believe that my mom is watching me now as I write these words to you. I believe that she is finally hearing me. Soul to soul she is hearing me, and it means so much to me. I pray the words of Ho'oponopono and feel an enormous amount of understanding take place as I do. I never believed that I was enough for my adoptive mother. Sitting here now and speaking the words *I love you. I'm sorry. Please forgive me. Thank you*, I finally have realized that I am. I am enough. I didn't do that. The divine did.

My first mother left this earth in July 2019. She was home, in England, when she died. I was in my birth country of England too but made the choice not to be physically present with my mum. Just a few short months before her death, she and I had a beautiful telephone conversation on her birthday. It was a pure, real, and loving conversation — so much so that I grabbed a notepad and wrote down all her words as she spoke them. Somehow I knew that we'd never have that kind of conversation again, or any conversation. I didn't want to forget her words or how they made me feel.

Mum was slipping further and further into dementia, but during our phone call she was very clear. She told me that she loved me and that she wanted me to know just how strong we both were, how strong we both had been. As I started to cry, she said, as she had said to me so many times over the years once we had reunited, "Not to worry, love. Not to worry."

As my first mother's dementia worsened, she had become more agitated and irritated. When I learned that she was near her transition into the next life, I couldn't bring myself to take the chance of having her lash out at me, and that's why I chose not to go to her.

I stayed in London and waited by the phone for news. As I waited, I prayed the words of Ho'oponopono. *I love you. I'm sorry. Please forgive me. Thank you.*

I asked the divine to hear my words as I said, "I love you, Mum. I'm sorry I'm not there in the hospital with you. Yet I am here in England and near you. Please forgive me for not being there. I don't want you to feel left by me, but I know you will understand. Our last conversation was such a gift, and the words you spoke were from your heart and soul. Your words represented the best of us. It is those words and the love they carry that I want to keep with me. Thank you for our conversation last October. Thank you for speaking those healing words to me. Your words mothered me. I do believe that was your intention. I love you. I'm sorry. Please forgive me. Thank you."

As I spoke those words, there in my birth country of England, I received notification that my Mum had passed away. The family had left the room and there was no one with her. No one but my spiritual presence and the prayer of Ho'oponopono. I believe that Mum felt my spirit and my words. She took her last breath when she could feel that all was back in balance between us. I didn't do that. The divine did.

I love you. I'm sorry. Please forgive me. Thank you.

CONCLUSION

I Believe in These Words, and I Believe in You

I hope you will speak the words of Ho'oponopono and begin to note any shifts that you experience as you do. Don't overthink this process; just lean into it and allow the words to open you up to a place of peace within. Take notice of the shifts in your internal world and how these shifts impact your external world. Let yourself feel love and gratitude as you make this practice a part of your daily ritual. I believe in the power of these words of Ho'oponopono. I believe in the power of you.

As you move forward in your life, please return to these chapters as reminders of all that you are capable of healing, all that you are capable of becoming. And don't underestimate the shifts — even if subtle — that have occurred so far as you've made your way through this book and explored the exercises, meditations, and affirmations. These are not designed for one-time use — they are here to support you, day in and day out.

Acknowledge and celebrate the fact that you didn't avoid the directives in these pages (even if you might have at first!), even when it might have been uncomfortable to face the feelings that arose. You remained here, with me, and stayed true to yourself, receptive in the midst of hard truths and willing while facing the triggers and the fear. Your courageous and resourced adult self, along with the knowledge that you are divinely guided, have led you here to the final pages of this book. Your journey is just beginning, though. Honor that!

Please hear me when I say that it doesn't matter if you haven't completely shifted a behavior pattern or transformed a limiting belief at this point. Be gentle with yourself, and remember that what matters most is that you've been courageous in exploring what awaits beneath the pain points you've identified. You've reconnected to yourself along this journey of adoptee reclamation, and you've done the challenging work of excavation as you've gone deep to discover truth and a deeper sense of acceptance and self-love.

You've stayed curious as you've turned each page, and you've sat bravely within each awakening that's happened for you. Step-by-step and moment by moment, you've moved closer to the truth of who you are and to the truth of what the adoptee experience means for you. You're realigning with your truth, and each subtle shift will continue to move you closer to your truest nature and identity. And, with every loving and healing breath that you take, you are moving closer to that greater vision for yourself and your life.

I've shared so much of my truth as an adoptee in these pages, along with the truths of other adoptees, in the hope that you will know you're not alone. Our paths, as adoptees, are not meant to look exactly the same, and neither is our healing journey. I do pray, however, that this book will inspire you to put into practice one or more of these healing approaches so that you can feel more and more empowered — more and more connected to yourself.

Relinquishment, rejection, abandonment, and adoption loss are all traumatic life experiences. I am so proud of your commitment to look at these tough places and do the soulful work of initiating a healing that can move you forward. I'm so grateful and intensely proud that you would pick up this book as a way to learn more about the thoughts and feelings that come with living as an adoptee. I'm in awe of you for staying open to these alternative methods of healing and for seeing the value in soul work. Every awakening, no matter how big or small, that has been ignited within you through reading this book is a miracle and a gift.

I believe in your healing and in your ability to free yourself from the sticky residue of rejection. I know it's hard to believe that someone out there really understands your pain, but I do. Even though you may be holding this book hundreds of miles away from where I am, an energy — an electricity — is being exchanged within these pages. It's a powerful force! And I hope that at some point you recognized a bit of yourself in me and a moment of your journey in mine. We are that connected. The pain may be great right now, but I assure you that the love is greater.

I want you to know that I'm rooting for you. I'm cheering you on, every step along this journey as adopted people. You also have a host of angelic ancestors surrounding you and loving you. You have a loving Creator who wants you to realize all that you're here to be beyond the pain and the hurt.

Let us, as adoptees, see a vaster way forward. May we realize greatness in ourselves and in each other. May we take the vision and create a better reality for our today and for all our tomorrows. I hope you'll take this moment with me and close your eyes to connect with this vision.

- Gently place your hands on your heart.
- Take a deep breath in, then exhale.
- Continue to breathe in and out.
- Say to yourself: I love you. I'm sorry. Please forgive me. Thank you.

Sit quietly for a moment and feel the energy of these words. Feel the energy of my love. Contemplate that you are here — living and breathing — despite the many challenges and roadblocks of the adoptee experience. This should be solid proof of the kind of champion you are, one who shows up in service of your own rescue and, in so doing, rescues others by your example.

Adoption is not the sum of who you are, although I know it's a part of your life journey, and will continue to be. Through your healing work, the many other parts of you will emerge. Celebrate each and every part, and continue to give yourself permission to heal and to grow and to become. I believe in you. I believe in us. I believe in every adoptee. Let us be greater. Let us be. Let us.

Adoptee Affirmation

The light around me is great, but the light within me is greater.

Acknowledgments

I am deeply thankful to Georgia Hughes for her kind support and her keen insights in the transformation of my manuscript into this book and for illuminating it into the world. It is a pure honor to work with her. I extend my appreciation to everyone at New World Library. Their warm welcome and belief in this book has been a gift.

My forever gratitude goes to my literary agent, Stephanie Tade, who kept the light on and guided this book home. She believes in the transformational power of story and helped this book find its wings. My thanks to my book proposal coach, Richelle Fredson, who saw the vision and need for this book early on and mentored me in the crafting of a blueprint that was meaningful and heartfelt.

I am also thankful to everyone who housed me, fed me, and wished me well as I wrote this book. Thank you to those who offered their feedback, both early on and in the later stages of the publishing process.

Finally, I want to express my love and gratitude to my family. I am nothing without you. To my Creator, whose unfailing grace amazes me. To my spiritual teachers and coaches who have helped me heal my life as an adoptee, I thank you for sharing your wisdom with me. To my parents — first, foster, and adoptive — I thank you for the lessons. And, to adoptees around the world, I am incredibly proud to stand with you. This book is for you.

Notes

Introduction

p. 5   *Every part of your existence*: Ashley Foster, "Darryl McDaniels, DMC of Run-D.M.C., Discovers His Adoption Story," Adoption.com, July 13, 2017, https://adoption.com/darryl-mcdaniels -run-dmc-adoption.

Chapter One: Labeled and Lessened

p. 23   *Once the child is conceived*: Bruce Lipton, *The Biology of Belief: Unleashing the Power of Consciousness, Matter & Miracles*, 10th anniversary ed. (Carlsbad, CA: Hay House, 2005), 182.

p. 24   *In fact, the great weight of the scientific evidence*: Thomas R. Verny and Pamela Weintraub, *Pre-parenting: Nurturing Your Child from Conception* (New York: Simon & Schuster, 2002), 29.

p. 24   *If the mother is under stress*: Lipton, *Biology of Belief*, 183.

p. 24   *Stress hormones prepare the body*: Lipton, *Biology of Belief*, 183.

p. 24   *Scientific research now reveals*: Bryan Post, "The Adopted Child: Trauma and Its Impact," Post Institute, November 6, 2013, https://postinstitute.com/the-adopted-child-trauma-and-its -impact.

p. 25   *The lesson for adoptive parents*: Lipton, *Biology of Belief*, 190.

p. 26   *Deep within all of us*: Gabrielle Bernstein, *Happy Days: The Guided Path from Trauma to Profound Freedom and Inner Peace* (Carlsbad, CA: Hay House, 2022), 4.

Chapter Three: Permission to Grieve

p. 62   *Sit with this sobering statistic*: Margaret A. Keyes et al., "The Risk
          of Suicide Attempt in Adopted and Nonadopted Offspring,"
          Pediatrics 132, no. 4 (Oct. 2013): 639–46, doi: 10.1542/peds
          .2012-3251.

p. 62   *The meta-analysis conducted*: Ryan Gustafsson and Patricia
          Fronek, "Intercountry Adoption and Suicide in Australia: A
          Scoping Review," Australian Government, Department of
          Social Services, 2022, https://www.dss.gov.au/sites/default/files
          /documents/02_2023/intercountry-adoption-and-suicide
          -australia-scoping-review.pdf.

Chapter Nine: Realigning with the Light of Transparency and Acceptance

p. 183   *Spiritual pioneers*: Eckhart Tolle, *The Power of Now: A Guide
          to Spiritual Enlightenment* (Novato, CA: New World Library,
          1999), 4.

Chapter Ten: The Light of Forgiveness and Clearing Inner Blocks

p. 193   *I first read about this practice*: Jim Vitale and Ihaleakala Hew
          Len, *Zero Limits: The Secret Hawaiian System for Health, Wealth,
          Peace, and More*, 1st ed. (New York: Wiley, 2008).

About the Author

M ichelle Madrid is a life coach and guidance mentor who is passionate about igniting the light within every adoptee. She seeks soulful modalities of healing to support clients in feeling a deeper connectedness with themselves and with others.

Michelle is a former foster child from the United Kingdom and an international adoptee. She understands the nuances of the adoptee experience and considers it a great honor to guide adoptees back home to themselves as they embrace a deeper sense of identity and calling.

Michelle is a Congressional Coalition on Adoption Institute (CCAI) Angels in Adoption Honoree as well as an inductee to the New Mexico Women's Hall of Fame. She is a former Emmy-nominated television news journalist and an in-demand high-impact speaker whose perspectives are renowned both domestically and internationally. She is also the host of the *Electricity of You* podcast, sharing transformational teachings that nudge listeners to respark their potential. Her illuminating content and coaching offerings can be found at TheMichelleMadrid.com.

Michelle is a mother by adoption and birth. She's an animal lover, passionate equestrian, and a world traveler who feels at home no matter where she is because she's found her home within.

TheMichelleMadrid.com